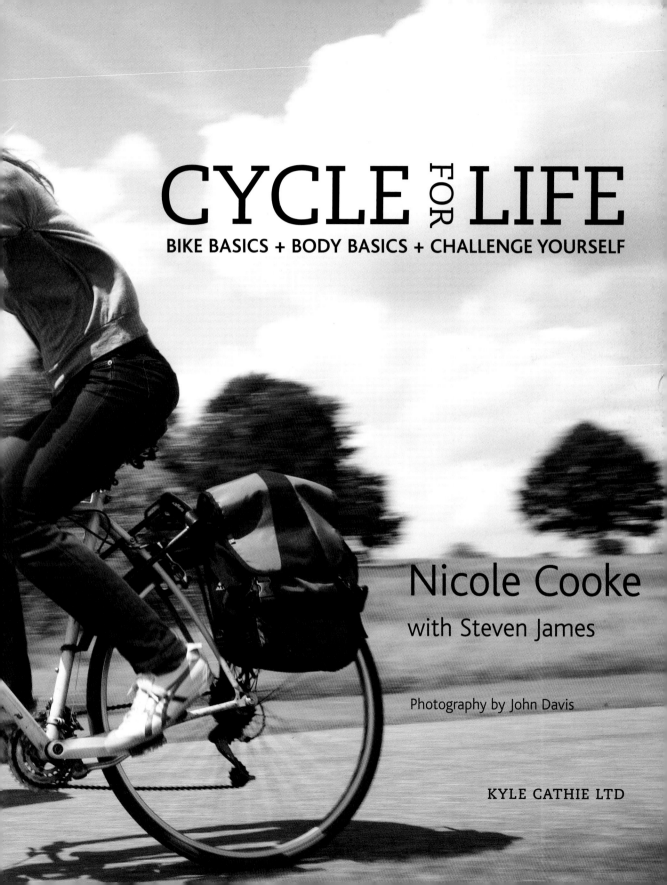

CYCLE FOR LIFE

BIKE BASICS + BODY BASICS + CHALLENGE YOURSELF

Nicole Cooke

with Steven James

Photography by John Davis

KYLE CATHIE LTD

First published in Great Britain in 2008 by
Kyle Cathie Limited
122 Arlington Road
London NW1 7HP
general.enquiries@kyle-cathie.com
www.kylecathie.com

ISBN 978 1 85626 756 4

Project Editor: Danielle Di Michiel
Designer: Carl Hodson
Copy Editor and Indexer: Ann Kingdom
Photography: John Davis
Production: Sha Huxtable
Models: Nicole Cooke, Simon Hammonds
and Catherine Heygate

A Cataloguing in Publication record for this title is available
from the British Library.

Printed and bound in Singapore by Tien Wah Press

CONTENTS

Nicole Cooke

INTRODUCTION

Roaring down an exhilarating descent, riding through forests, along coasts or across cities, or cresting a hill and discovering a beautiful view – these are just some of the reasons why I love cycling and decided to follow my dreams of being a professional cyclist.

Since beginning racing at the age of eleven, I have had the opportunity to travel to many different countries and experience at first hand what nature has to offer. I have been discovering new roads under my own natural power and strength in my quest to become the best cyclist I can be. Through racing I have pitted myself against the best riders in the world, on some of the hardest terrain, and had the pleasure of that winning feeling when tactics and physical strength combine in perfect harmony to deliver me to the finishing line before the others!

In this time I have reached the top of the world rankings, winning major championships and World Cup titles along the way. I have studied many books and training manuals, taken advice from some of the most knowledgeable experts, and learned a few lessons of my own – sometimes the hard way.

Aside from my racing achievements I know that cycling will always play a part in my life. Some of my earliest memories are of playing on a bike or going 'exploring'. It gave me the freedom to go where my heart wanted to take me, but under the cover of the silence that a bike can give I always felt as though I was meant to be part of nature. The bike is just a machine but it's almost majestic when you're riding at full power and full speed. Whether you're commuting, racing or enjoying a trip out with friends or family, you can relish the experience, knowing there is no harm to nature and that you're also investing in your own health and a happy future.

I hope you enjoy this book as a guide to cycling. The chapters are written to help you get started and then guide you through the different stages of cycling development. If you're new to cycling, I hope this book will help you to begin safely and with confidence and incorporate it into your everyday life. If you're already a regular cyclist, I hope that by the time you have finished reading this book you will have benefited from the insights and tips I have picked up throughout my career, and that you will be more knowledgeable and better able to get everything you want out of cycling.

Whatever stage you're at, and whatever your goals, I hope the experience and research I have put into this book will help you to reach new heights, whether you're aiming for a healthy lifestyle, looking for fresh challenges or venturing into racing and the ultimate test of speed and strength.

Good Luck!
Nicole Cooke

52 REASONS TO RIDE

There are all sorts of reasons why people want to ride, need to ride or just love to ride. Here are enough for every single week of the year, and I'm sure you can think of more!

1 You get great views from a bike.

2 Fresh air clears your mind – and the sheer pleasure of riding a bike reduces stress, anxiety and depression.

3 You can get closer to nature and wildlife, at home and abroad, with the silence of a bike – you can see, hear and smell more.

4 Cycling is the most efficient method of transport – it uses about 20 per cent of the energy needed to walk the same distance.

5 A bike can last a lifetime if you look after it and maintain it properly.

6 Cycling strengthens your whole body – it uses your back and upper body as well as strengthening and toning your legs, and benefits your cardiovascular system too.

7 Through your cycling achievements, you can inspire others to overcome their own challenges.

8 Cycling is great for rehabilitation following injuries in other sports – it's non-weight-bearing and has a low impact on your joints.

9 Cycling is a social activity – you can enjoy riding as a group and sharing your experiences, or even start a blog or a website about your travels, your adventures or just your mileage.

10 Share your cycling experience with the family on tandems by fitting child seats.

11 Challenge yourself to reach your personal best or race others to express your competitive streak!

12 Gain mental benefits by learning to set yourself goals and enjoy the self-confidence that comes with achieving them, or at least learning along the way.

13 Save money on gym membership – get a work-out before and after your day at the office by commuting to work.

14 There's so much variety in cycling – on-road, off-road, single tracks, fire tracks, downhills, velodromes, freestyle, BMX ...

15 Cycling is a cheap mode of transport – bikes cost a fraction of the price of cars and motorbikes to buy and to maintain and repair (and you save on city-centre parking costs).

16 Cycling is often the fastest mode of transport in cities, especially during the rush hour – four million people in Beijing can't be wrong!

17 Cycling can make train travel easier if you use a bike to get to or from the station – consider getting a folding bike if you make a lot of train journeys.

18 Travel the world. Cycling is a global sport with races, Sportives or simply just roads everywhere!

19 Cycle-friendly companies and employers can make better use of their land by having bike spaces instead of car parks – six to twenty bikes can fit in the space needed for just one car.

20 Cycling is good for you and for the environment.

21 Get to know your town or city better by taking to it on a bike.

22 Cycling can help weight loss – every hour of moderate-intensity cycling burns around 400 calories.

23 Meet new people through cycling groups and clubs.

24 Now you don't need to think of an excuse to get into lycra!

25 Colour co-ordinate your bike and kit to reflect your personality or mood.

26 Ride the same routes as the heroes of the Tour de France.

27 Racing can allow you to play to your competitive strengths, whether it is teamwork or being the leader for a race.

28 Teamwork through organising cycling trips or riding as a team in races are valuable skills employers look for.

29 Charity rides allow you to give something to charity while you keep fit and enjoy it at the same time.

30 One day you could become a coach or mentor and pass on your experiences to help other newcomers to cycling.

31 You can learn about the physiological effects of training or do research into them.

32 Helps your sun-tan and positive energy from being out in the sun.

33 Learning bicycle maintenance and other mechanical skills helps to give you a better understanding of how machines and technology work.

34 Cycling gives children their first sense of independence.

35 Cycling fosters self-reliance through being the one person in control of events.

36 Learn to problem solve or adapt to scenarios or changes in plan out on the road.

37 People of all ages can cycle – low forces encourage longevity in cycling.

38 Ditch the air-con and enjoy a natural breeze on a bike to keep you cool on summer days.

39 Reduce your chances of getting sick and save on health costs by being fitter and more active – cycling 20 miles (32km) a week can reduce the risk of heart disease to less than half that of people who do no exercise.

40 Enjoy the feeling of swapping your training bike or wheels for your race bike ... you'll feel like you're flying!

41 Become better prepared for rides on the pedalo at theme parks or on holiday!

42 Cycling strength crosses over into so many other sports, whether it is the strength side or endurance side.

43 You can't beat the feeling of achievement of climbing that hill or mountain....

44 Unless you have just climbed it faster....

45 Or you're just about to start the descent....

46 Learn about the science behind the sport – aerodynamics and some of the basics of physics.

47 Choose a different route every day, or enjoy doing the same route faster.

48 Races include a mixture of body, brain and bike ... not just one element!

49 Combine visiting friends or relatives with cycling or racing in new areas or regions.

50 Have cost-efficient holidays – cycling is a faster alternative than backpacking if you take your camping and other supplies with you in panniers on your carriers.

51 Combine a holiday with racing – visit Italy and ride Gran Fondos.

52 Choose the races that suit you best – sprints, hill climbing, track or mountain biking. You can always change discipline and still be cycling.

You've decided you want to start cycling, but what do you need to do next? There are a number of things you need to know before you get riding. Most importantly, which bike is best for you? This is an individual choice, influenced by any number of factors including cost, level of fitness and necessity.

In this section you'll find out which bikes suit which riders, and any other equipment you'll need to get started. I'll take you through the mechanics of your new bike and how it all works together to get you where you want to go.

PART ONE

BIKE BASICS

1: THE BIKE

To some people their bike is just a workhorse to get them from A to B. For others it's a prized possession, a treasured friend or even a work of art! Some bikes are really cheap, while some cost thousands. Different styles of bikes are suited to different kinds of cycling.

Understanding the different parts of a bike, how to use them and how to look after them, will provide you with a better, and safer, experience.

HOW IT WORKS

A bike has up to 3,000 parts which work together with your own body and natural forces to create a harmonious system, and one of the most efficient methods of getting from one place to another. It starts with the downward force that your legs and feet apply to the pedals. This is converted through a series of levers, chains and sprockets into the force that turns your rear wheel, and the traction of your rear tyre on the road propels your bike forwards.

Of course you must also prevent the bike from toppling over! You do this by making subtle, almost imperceptible, small corrections through gentle steering or leaning slightly. This may sound difficult or complicated, but once you have mastered the act of cycling it becomes second nature – it's one of the skills that will remain with you for life!

The photograph shows the bike and its components, all of which can be changed or adjusted, depending on your position and riding needs.

Frame

1: Top tube
2: Down tube
3: Seat stays
4: Chain stays

5: Bottom bracket
6: Forks

Front wheel

7: Tyre
8: Spokes
9: Rim
10: Hub

11: Rear wheel

12: Sprockets/cassette
13: Handlebar stem
14: Handlebars
15: Saddle
16: Seat pin
17: Pedals
18: Cranks
19: Chain ring
20: Chain
21: Gear lever
22: Cables
23: Rear derailleur
24: Front derailleur
25: Brakes
26: Brake calliper
27: Drop-outs

THE FRAME

The frame is the 'skeleton' that supports the whole bike system. It is a lightweight structure that has to be strong enough to support your weight and stiff enough to allow the efficient transmission of power into forward motion, while also having some degree of flexibility to absorb the bumps and shocks that are transmitted up from the road. The size and fit of your frame will influence how you feel and how you ride your bike. Frames are made from various materials; sometimes two or more are combined to achieve particular combinations of strength and lightness.

Carbon Fibre: Increasingly the most common material for road or race frames, carbon fibre is super-light and super-stiff. These frames are good at absorbing shocks from the road, but they can crack or break if twisted.

Titanium: This is very strong, so titanium frames can be made with extremely thin tubing, making them very lightweight. Originally used in rockets or aeroplanes, titanium frames are comfortable and long lasting, but they can be expensive.

Steel: For a comfortable ride, steel frames can be a good all-round choice. Steel is not the lightest material, but by building frames from tubes of different thicknesses, depending on where the strength is needed, very good cost-effective frames can be made.

Aluminium: This is very light but is usually a very soft material. The key to a good aluminium frame is the correct thickness of tubing, good welding and the right frame geometry, which can make the frame super-stiff. This makes aluminium frames very efficient for racers wanting to turn all their efforts into maximum speed, but they can give a harsh or uncomfortable ride, especially if you spend long hours in the saddle.

Hybrid frames: Although you will find frames made exclusively from one of these materials, you will also find hybrid models. For instance, the larger front triangle of the bike might be made from aluminium to make it stiff and efficient, with the chain stays and seat stays made from carbon fibre to add a little extra comfort.

FORKS

The forks are very important for the steering and handling of your bike. The rake or angle of the forks determines the bike's sharpness and responsiveness, and a fork made out of stiff materials will help to transfer more of your power into speed.

Suspension forks

Many mountain bikes have a front or rear suspension system which aims to take out the rough shocks and bumps from off-road terrain. This gives you a more comfortable ride and helps increase traction as you deliver power smoothly to the pedals – hopefully making you faster.

HEADSET

The headset is the connection between frame, forks and handlebars, and makes it possible to steer the bike. There are many different designs and you must have a headset that is compatible with your frame and forks. Sealed cartridges, ball bearings or roller-and-needle bearings are used for a smooth movement, with steering and headsets falling into four main categories: A-head or threadless, integrated, semi-integrated and threaded.

HANDLEBARS

The handlebars support your hands and arms and steer the bike, as they are directly connected to the steering column that runs from the top of the forks up through the head-tube of the frame to where the handlebar stem attaches. Handlebars can be made of steel, carbon fibre or aluminium, and there are many different styles in different widths, with different drops and grip sizes. Your preference will depend on the size and shape of your hands and your style of cycling.

Traditional dropped handlebars

These give you a variety of options for where to put your hands, depending on your riding position. This helps to reduce unnecessary stress on your arms, shoulders and back. You can hold the tops to maximise efficiency when climbing, but the hooks are great for descending, cornering, sprinting or riding at speed, where you can make the most of the lower aerodynamic position. You can also hold the brake hoods if you're riding out of the saddle or need to brake quickly when riding in traffic or difficult conditions

Mountain bike handlebars

These bars are wider than dropped handlebars, and they are either straight or have a slight 'rise', which gives you a lot of control and better handling for off-road riding. Bar ends can be added to mountain bikes to give you another option for holding and controlling the bike. Some city bikes or commuter bikes use straight or slightly 'bucket-handle' handlebars.

Aero or tri-bars

These are specifically designed to make you as aerodynamic as possible, with your hands and elbows close together, and can be very low to reduce the amount of drag created by your frontal area. They are used in time trials, pursuits and triathlon and are only suited to solo riding as it's difficult to brake quickly or see where you're going if you use them when you're in a group of riders.

CONTROL LEVERS

Many bikes have gear shifters that are integrated into the brake lever so you can have more control when slowing down and changing gear and don't have to change your hand position. They are dual control on most road bikes, and on mountain bikes you can also find grip-shift or rapid-fire gear controls. Control levers are built specifically for the number of chain rings and number of sprockets on your bike. Practice makes perfect; once you're used to them, they can give you great control and confidence when riding.

BRAKES

Road bikes have rim brakes as specified by the rules of the International Cycling Union (UCI) for racing bikes. A cable runs from the brake lever to a set of callipers, usually via a side-pull mechanism. Rim brakes used on off-road bikes are V-brakes, which have high side arms and create higher brake forces than road callipers. (The higher the side arms, the higher the braking force.) Cantilever brakes are a little weaker than V-brakes and have a centre-pull system, with the brake cable connected to a bridge cable, which then pulls both arms of the brake at the same time. These have traditionally been used on bikes designed for touring. Some touring bikes may have brakes that use a hydraulic system.

Disk brakes give the strongest braking forces by converting more of your force at the brake lever into stopping power at the disk. They are hydraulic or cable operated.

TRANSMISSION

Transforming your pedalling into forward motion is taken care of by the transmission. This consists of the gear mechanisms, the chain rings, the cassette or sprockets, the cranks and the bottom bracket.

Crankset: The crankset transfers the force you push down on the pedals to the back wheel, via the chain. Cranks can be made of a variety of materials with different qualities, creating a huge range of designs and lengths.

Chain ring: The two cranks are joined together by a bottom bracket through the joint at the bottom of the frame and connected to the chain ring. Track bikes have a single chain ring, as usually do time-trial bikes. Road racing bikes tend to have two chain rings, while Sportive, touring, hybrid and mountain bikes tend to have 'a triple'.

Gears: The gear ratio that you ride in is expressed as the relationship between the number of teeth on your chain ring and the size of the cog or sprocket you have selected on the cassette attached to your rear wheel. The front gear-changing mechanism, attached to the seat tube, along with the rear derailleur mechanism, guides the chain into the correct position for the gear ratio you have chosen.

WHEELS

The hubs, spokes and wheel rims fit together to support the rider and the bike and they take all the force from the road as the wheels turn. The bearings in the hubs need to be as smooth and efficient as possible so that all the energy delivered to the sprockets goes into turning the wheels. Wheels need to be stiff so that they do not flex under the load, and spokes and rims can be made from different materials and in different designs to make them as fast and efficient as possible.

TYRES

The tyres and their tread are very specific to the terrain over which you intend to ride. Thin tyres with a low rolling resistance are great for speed, wider tyres with a little more grip and puncture resistance are good for touring and commuting, while off-road tyres have an endless combination of widths and tread for all kinds of terrain and weather conditions.

TIP

Check the direction of your tyre's tread! Some tyres have directional tread to help you go forwards faster.

TIP

You may actually have the right saddle, just the wrong position. Try adjusting the height, set-back and angle to change the weight distribution between your handlebars and saddle.

SADDLE

The choice of saddle is very personal to each cyclist. Along with the pedals and handlebars, the saddle is one of the three contact points between you and your bike. What is perfect for one person may not be comfortable for another, given the body's sensitivity in this area, with different people having varying amounts of soft tissue and muscle and differently shaped bones.

Saddles come in various shapes, widths, lengths, colours and materials, as well as with different amounts of padding. They can also have special features like holes cut out of the middle of the saddle and pressure-point gel inserts. There are also raised pelvic seats and ladies' saddles. You may need to try a few saddles before finding the one that is just right for you.

PEDALS

Traditional flat (or platform) pedals are common for leisure bikes and for BMX and freeride bikes. These can have toe-clips attached to give you the option of a more fixed foot position, providing a more powerful pedalling stroke.

There is also the clip-less option, a specially designed pedal with a unique cleat which attaches to the sole of your cycling shoe. This allows you to transfer power to the pedals very efficiently and makes it easy to clip them in or out when starting and stopping. There are many designs available. Road pedals tend to have a bigger platform for better power transfer, but this also means bigger cleats, which are sometimes tricky for walking. Off-road pedals are designed to work even with a build-up of mud, and have smaller, recessed cleats, which allow you to walk or run off-road too. The pedal mechanism can have some 'float' or movement, allowing your foot to find its most natural position, or it can be fixed. It can take a little while and some trial and error to find the best cleat position for your body.

TIP

A narrow saddle tends to be better for long rides, allowing you to pedal efficiently without rubbing the inside of your legs against it. You can also slide forwards and backwards to relieve different areas during the course of your ride. Wider saddles tend to have more padding, making them softer, but they tend to keep you fixed in one position.

BUYING A BIKE

Before buying a bike you have several important things to consider, including your budget and the kind of cycling you will be doing.

- Generally, if you aim to do a mixture of different kinds of cycling, a mountain bike is a great way to start; it can take you off onto the trails and mountains but also get you from A to B on roads or bike paths quickly and safely.
- If you know that you're going to be doing long rides on tarmac, tackling mountain climbs and doing long-distance tests of endurance, then a road bike is the best option.
- If you're thinking of commuting, then a bike that can take the daily beating of the miles and cope with different seasons of the year will serve you best.

If you're still undecided, you could err on the side of caution and start by getting an economically priced bike within your budget. This will help you to start cycling. Once you've had some experience you will have a better idea of the kind of bike that will suit your riding requirements, whether it be a super-lightweight road model, a sturdy tourer or a full-suspension mountain bike. Your first all-round bike will still be good enough to use as a spare or a training bike alongside your new one, especially as the equipment is likely to be more durable and cheaper to replace than that of a top-specification bike.

If possible, test ride the bike to get a feel of how it handles and whether or not you find it comfortable. Check the guarantee and remember that a good cycle shop or retailer should have an after-sales support service for any adjustments that may be needed once you start riding the bike regularly.

FIT YOUR BIKE

Most of us rode a bike when we were children, and even if you haven't sat on one for years there's nothing to it, is there? After all, as they say, 'It's just like riding a bike!' That may be true, but whether your aim is to maximise enjoyment or improve performance there's a little more to it than just throwing your leg over and turning the pedals. Making sure your bike is a good fit for your body will not only make it a more comfortable experience but will also help you ride much more efficiently and safely.

Later in the book we'll talk in more detail about how to set up your bike for performance, but first let's start with the basics (sometimes overlooked even by experienced riders).

FACT

Cycling was one of the first sports introduced in the Olympics in 1896 and is one of only five sports that have been in every modern Olympics.

Keep your shoulders and neck relaxed.

Your back should be comfortable. Adjust the height of your bars if you feel discomfort.

You should be sitting so that you can push strongly through the whole of the downstroke.

Your legs and knees should never feel as if they are over-stretching at the bottom of the stroke or being crushed at the top.

You should always try to look about 50m (55 yards) in front of you.

Your arms should be sloping forward, but not stretched.

Your hands should be relaxed, able to reach brakes and gears quickly and easily.

Your feet should normally be horizontal, and usually straight, pointing forwards on the pedals. Use your ankles to help keep your pedalling action smooth.

SADDLE POSITION

You can adjust the height, set-back and angle of your saddle. As a general rule, when you're sitting on the saddle and your leg is at the bottom of the range of motion, your knee should be slightly bent and your foot should be horizontal. Make sure you set this up wearing the shoes you use for cycling.

Most bikes are set up with the saddle 4–5cm (1.5–2in.) behind the vertical line to the bottom bracket, but if you're long limbed, or do a lot of endurance riding, you may want to try sliding the saddle further back. If, on the other hand, you have a more punchy pedalling style, or do a lot of short, intense rides, then you may want to try having the saddle a little further forward.

Usually the saddle will be horizontal, but as we'll explain later (p. 149), in some circumstances you may prefer to ride with the nose of the saddle sloping gently downwards.

HANDLEBAR POSITION

Choose a width of bar that is roughly the same width as your shoulders. If the bars are too narrow you will restrict your breathing by closing your ribcage. If they are too wide you may feel as if you have less control over the steering, and your frontal area will be much wider than it needs to be, increasing your air resistance! The length of your stem depends on the length of your top tube and personal riding style, but if your knees hit your elbows when you're pedalling, then it's too short, and if you can't reach the brakes and gears easily it's too long.

CAN YOU TOUCH YOUR TOES?

The height of the handlebars depends on the type of bike you have, the kind of riding you are going to do and how flexible your back is. To find the best height, try bending over to touch your toes, while keeping your legs straight.

- If you struggle to touch your toes, then you should start with your handlebars higher than your saddle.
- If you can touch your toes, try having your bars at a similar height to your saddle.
- If you can put the back of your fingers or palms on the floor, you could set your handlebars lower than your saddle.

Everyone is unique, so every rider must try to find the best position for themselves. Your height, the relative length of your legs compared to your trunk, the flexibility of your back and other muscles, as well as your individual riding style will all be specific to you and so you must try to find what is most comfortable. The same is also true for different bikes: a mountain bike will handle differently from a road bike, and so you must adjust your position depending on the type of bike and the kind of riding you will be doing. You may also find you gradually change your position as you become fitter.

2:KIT YOURSELF OUT

The bike and its components are not the only equipment that you need to think about to get the most out of cycling. Using the right clothing can make the experience much safer and much more comfortable, and it can even make you faster!

CLOTHING FOR DIFFERENT CONDITIONS

Whether you're enjoying the freedom of the open air or pushing your body to its natural limits, environmental conditions can also have a significant impact on your ride. Wearing appropriate clothing will make you more comfortable and help your body to perform to the best of its ability.

WARM-WEATHER CLOTHING
In temperatures above 20°C your clothing needs to be lightweight so you can stay as cool as possible and lose sweat easily:

- Lycra™ shorts with padded insert or chamois to help prevent saddle sores or chaffing
- Under-jersey made from material that absorbs or removes sweat from the skin. These fabrics, such as Nike's 'dri-fit', have a variety of brand names
- Jersey with rear pockets and a full-length zip so you can make adjustments, depending on how much air you need to cool you down
- Lightweight socks
- Mitts or gloves, to protect your hands and help you keep a good grip if your hands become sweaty
- Sweat band, bandana and cap

An important element of cycle clothing is to use a layer system. You can add or remove layers as the temperature goes up or down, so you don't need completely different wardrobes to cope with the weather in different seasons. On the bike, too, layers can help. You may start your ride wearing an extra top layer and leg- or arm-warmers, and then stash them in your pockets as you warm up.

TIP
Use sunscreen. Remember that areas such as the back of your neck are very exposed when riding in the sun. The sun can even get through some jerseys and shorts if they are made with 'tea bag' fabrics.

COLD-WEATHER CLOTHING

In colder conditions, you will need all or most of the following:

- Thermal undervest
- Thermal or airblock jersey
- Gilet/body warmer
- Arm-warmers and leg/knee-warmers
- Tights or airblock tights
- Thermal socks
- Over-shoes
- Thermal gloves
- Balaclava or scarf to keep cold air out of your lungs
- Hat/cap

WET-WEATHER CLOTHING

Whatever the season, cyclists usually need to be prepared for rain:

- Rain jacket, ideally one that stops rain coming in and lets sweat out, through material or through vents
- Waterproof socks
- Waterproof over-shoes
- Waterproof gloves

If you're commuting or touring you may wish to use waterproof over-trousers, or a traditional waterproof cycling cape that will keep you and even part of the bike well covered.

HELMETS

In some countries cycling helmets are compulsory, in others they are not. For racing and many other organised events it is mandatory to wear them. I always put my helmet on, even for short journeys, and consider it to be a sensible safety measure.

You should buy a helmet that is the correct size for the circumference of your head. Most shops selling helmets will have measuring tapes to help. Different helmet manufacturers will have a different range of sizes, but all can then be adjusted further by a series of pads or internal straps. The straps should be adjusted so that they hold the helmet level on your head, covering your forehead but not blocking your line of sight when riding. Once you have adjusted the straps so that the helmet is in the right place and comfortable, you can cut the excess to a neat length to stop it flapping around.

Some helmets have the option of adding a visor, which can help to stop water or mud being sprayed into your eyes.

TT HELMETS

For solo time trials or timed track events, special 'tear-drop'-style helmets are permitted to help make the rider as aerodynamic as possible. These aim to create as little disturbance and drag to the airflow as possible and tend to be specific to your riding position. Try a few different styles to find out what feels and looks best for your 'low-profile' position.

GLASSES

Glasses or goggles are great for stopping flies or debris from going into your eyes when riding. Choose your lenses depending on the conditions in which you're riding: dark or reflective lenses for bright sunny conditions, and clear or bright lenses for cloudy or rainy days. You can also buy 'photochromic' lenses that automatically adjust to light conditions.

When buying glasses make sure the contact points (nose and ears) are secure and comfortable and consider purchasing a pair that are coated with an anti-fogging agent, or have adequate ventilation, to stop them from misting up.

SHOES

When you first start cycling you can ride in trainers. These will work with flat platform pedals with or without toe-clips attached. However, if you're taking advantage of clipless pedals, then choosing the right shoes and setting them up correctly is important. In fact it's vital, not just to get the most out of your pedal stroke, but also to make sure you don't develop knee problems.

Cycling shoes are very personal to you and your feet; you must find a pair that is comfortable for you. Consider their shape and the type of soles they have; stiffer soles transmit more power, but the lack of flexibility means that they do not allow your foot to change its position.

The closure also needs to feel comfortable; velcro, straps, ratchets, laces – or a combination of these – need to give you the confidence that your feet are secure but they must apply the pressure in the right places. If you start to feel that they are cutting off the circulation in your feet you may need a different system.

FITTING THE CLEATS

To pedal efficiently and comfortably the ball of your foot should be over the spindle of the pedal. Making sure the cleats on the bottom of your shoes are in the right place may take a little time, but it will be well worthwhile. Run your finger along from the ball of your foot to the inside, where the bone sticks out slightly. Mark this point on the outside of your shoe or use some tape to do so. This will now act as the centre point for your cleats so that the ball of your foot is in the correct position on the pedal.

Some pedals and cleats allow you to angle your foot on the pedal to the natural position you adopt when standing. Try to re-create this foot position with your cleats by changing the angle, if necessary, to find the optimum for you.

Pedals can give you some 'float' or movement around the axis point of the centre of the cleat-pedal, or they can be fixed. I would recommend trying a position with some movement to begin with and then you can gradually reduce the amount of movement if you feel it works better for you.

The first time you ride with clipless pedals you will need to spend some time getting used to how they feel and work. Ride around in an open area where you have room to practise putting your foot on the pedal and then removing it. To remove your foot, give a firm twist well in advance of when you need to stop. Then, when you're confident and out riding for the first time, you must try to think about removing your feet well before junctions or traffic lights. Eventually it will become second nature but the first few rides will need a little extra concentration as you get used to them.

3:RIDING SKILLS

Once your bike is set up, it's time to ride! In order to cycle confidently and efficiently there are a number of skills to master, but you'll find many of these come naturally and soon become second nature. Some of these skills relate to how you interact with the bike itself, others to how you adapt to external factors, such as terrain, weather, fellow riders or other road users.

USING THE GEARS

At its simplest, riding is using the pedals to go, the handlebars to set your course, and the brakes to stop. Most bikes also have one other major technical advantage to help you ride optimally in all situations – the gears.

The rider is the engine of the bike, providing the power to turn the pedals. Transferring this into forward motion is all related to the levers and gears that link your pedals and cranks to your sprockets and wheels. Knowing how to find the optimum pedalling cadence or rhythm will save you energy and win you speed! Ideally, try to ride with a cadence of 90–100rpm (see Tip opposite). This will help keep your pedalling momentum going and transfer power to the bike efficiently and without causing excessive fatigue.

If you use too small a gear, your legs will have trouble keeping up. They will spin too fast and you will also hear the chain go slack and catch again as the gears engage on each stroke. Use too big a gear, and even though you may be pushing very hard on the pedals, the momentum will be so slow that you will get tired very quickly. You may even find it impossible to turn the pedals if you're in too big a gear while going uphill.

As your speed and the terrain vary, don't be afraid to make frequent adjustments: change little and often, one or two gears at a time. With a well-maintained bike the gears should change smoothly without disturbing your pedalling rhythm. It just takes a quick click, and you should soon find that you'll often be changing gear almost without thinking about it.

If you're approaching a sudden change in gradient, like the start of a hill, or you're going over the summit to start a descent, change the rear gears first and then immediately change the chain ring. This may take a little bit of practice to get used to as it will seem strange at first. If you're about to begin a descent, you must start by going into a smaller gear and pedalling faster before changing into the larger chain ring. The opposite is the case when you suddenly need a smaller gear to start a climb: you should first change up into the smaller sprockets on the rear wheel, making you push a bigger gear for a moment, before immediately changing to the smaller chain ring.

Gearing can seem complicated and you may sometimes see gears referred to in inches. All you really need to know is that the 'gear' you're in is a ratio between the number of teeth on the large chain ring at the front (attached to the pedals), and the sprockets on the back wheel. Selecting a bigger chain ring will widen the difference in the number of teeth between the two. This means you travel further with every pedal stroke, which is of course a harder or 'bigger' gear. Choosing larger sprockets narrows the difference, so you travel a shorter distance for each spin of the pedals. This is an easier or 'smaller' gear.

Remember:
- If you feel yourself getting tired and your rate of pedalling is slowing down, change to a smaller gear which requires less force.
- If you're riding uphill, or into a head wind, and the resistance increases, change down to a smaller gear to use the power of your legs more efficiently.
- If you're accelerating, riding downhill, or with a tail wind, change up into a bigger gear so that you can use your energy more efficiently to ride at higher speeds.

Don't allow the chain to be at an angle across your chain rings and cassette. It is the mechanism for transmitting power to your back wheel and any extra resistance in the chain will slow you down. When climbing, you may be tempted to stay in the big ring and go down the gears. But as the chain moves to the bigger sprockets, so the tension on the chain and rear derailleur increases. The chain is designed to work in a straight line, but as the tension increases, it has to move under more and more sideways tension. This can cause you to lose as much as 15 per cent of your power. In extreme cases, the chain may suddenly jump off the chain ring, completely disrupting your rhythm or even causing you to lose control of the bike.

TIP

rpm = revolutions per minute. Some bicycle computers can display this. If yours doesn't, keep an eye on the clock and count how many times either your right or left foot pushes down in thirty seconds. Double this number and you have your rpm.

TIP

If you try to change both sprocket and ring at the same time there will be too much slack or too much tension in the chain, which may cause it to jump or bounce off the front ring. As you change ring you should also think about easing off pedalling slightly for half a revolution, to allow the chain to move easily and smoothly, before you put the pressure back on again.

BRAKING

Braking is an essential skill which riders don't always get right. Once again, however, the correct techniques are easily mastered with a little thought and practice. Do it correctly and not only will you be safer, but you won't waste energy needlessly.

First, stay relaxed. The brakes are powerful, and by squeezing the levers lightly to begin with you will soon realise how much force is needed to slow you down. Remember, at high speeds you will need to brake harder and need more distance to stop than when braking from slower speeds.

The front brake will give you more powerful braking performance but this can also work against you. If you pull too sharply it will move your body weight over the front wheel, possibly raising your back wheel or, worse still, causing you to go over the handlebars! Be careful not to over-use the front brake when descending hills as you may lose control or fall in corners.

TIP

If you do have to stop in an emergency, brake hard and move your weight back over the rear wheel. This will stop you going over the handlebars and give you more stability.

The back brake is good for steady braking and is more suitable for most cornering and descending situations. A light touch, braking progressively harder if necessary, is usually the best policy. Pulling too hard on the back brake may cause the tyre to skid. Not only is this not the quickest way to slow down, but you may also easily lose control. If your back wheel does lock up, and you have time to react, immediately let go of the back brake to allow the bike to stabilise and you to regain control, and then reapply the pressure for a smoother braking performance.

TIP
Practise!

CORNERING

Cornering is a skill with a number of factors involved, both before and during the manoeuvre. Preparation is the key here: ensure you approach the turn correctly. This will help you get through the bend quickly, safely and with the minimum fuss.

APPROACHING THE CORNER
As you approach a bend, look ahead and ask yourself several questions. How sharp is the corner? Can you see the exit? Is the road on a camber? Considering these factors will help you decide how much you need to reduce your speed, when and how hard to brake, and how much you may have to lean into the corner.

It's best to trim your speed to an appropriate pace before entering into the bend, though this isn't always possible. Move to the outside of the road as you approach the bend so that you can make the best possible use of the whole road (making sure, of course, that you obey traffic rules and stay on your own side of the carriageway if appropriate).

If the bend is to the right, then you should straighten your left leg to the 6 o'clock position, pushing down on the outside pedal. This will give you a stable platform as you lean into the corner. It will also mean that your inside pedal is at the 12 o'clock position, giving you maximum clearance as you lean into the bend and making sure you don't accidentally catch it on the floor. This is good practice for most corners, although in some shallow bends you may be able to continue pedalling right the way through.

INTO THE BEND
The next important aspect of cornering is choosing the right course. Look to the apex of the corner, where you want your bike to go, and lean in with your body, pushing down through your outside leg. If you're riding a bike with drop handlebars, then move your hands down low onto the bends. If you find you still need to take off some speed, try to use both the front and back brake together to give an even braking effect.

As you go through the apex of the corner, look to your exit route, moving towards the outside of the road, where you can keep as much speed as possible. Let go of the brakes and as your straighten up you can begin to pedal again.

Cornering correctly is one of the main skills needed when riding downhill, especially if you're trying to go as fast as possible. If you're descending a mountain pass, you may arrive at a corner very fast and have to brake to go round a hairpin bend or sharp corner. Changing down to a smaller gear just as you arrive will help you accelerate more quickly back to your top speed again.

If the corner is a sharp one or a hairpin bend, and you cannot see beyond it, always calculate your line and speed as if a car was approaching from the other direction. There is no point in risking your life to gain a few extra seconds on a downhill. If you find the corner is not as sharp as you expected, you can straighten up a little and start pedalling again to keep your speed up. On the other hand, if you find that the corner keeps on going and is sharper than you thought, apply some more even pressure to the brakes and keep leaning in with your body and keeping the pressure down through your outside leg.

CORNERING TECHNIQUES

Hands: Place your hands in the hooks of the bars. This helps keep your centre of gravity low in the corners, gives you good control of the bars, and helps you brake better, with more force, if needed.

Knees: As you go round the corner, the position of your inside leg can make a big difference to your speed and how safe you feel. One technique is to point your knee outwards (in the style of a motorbike rider) towards the ground. This will lower your centre of gravity. The other technique is to keep your outside leg firm against the frame of your bike, which will give you a lot more stability.

There is no right or wrong cornering technique; it's something you must try yourself as it depends on your riding style, your height and your bike set-up.

TIP

To adjust your line through a corner you don't need to turn your handlebars, just move your body weight. If you find you need to take a tighter line, just lean a little more to the inside of the bend. If you feel you want to take a wider line, just shift your weight to the outside and you will find your bike taking the corner less sharply.

FACT

On a bike you can travel three times faster than you can walk, for the same amount of energy.

CLIMBING

When you're riding on the flat you only have to overcome the friction of your wheels on the road or trail, and the resistance of the air you're moving through. Once the road goes up, you add another factor – gravity! Some people find they can fly up hills and love climbing, other riders find it a bit more of a challenge. Approaching climbs with a strategy will help you deal with this challenge in the most efficient way.

As with some of the other skills we've talked about, anticipation and preparation are the keys. Change down one or two gears as you approach a hill and keep your pedalling cadence high. Hold the bars in a comfortable way; there is little need for braking so choose a position that you're happy with, possibly further forward if the hill is steep and you need to keep more weight over the front wheel.

As the gradient steepens, change down to try and keep your cadence high, if possible. Some riders prefer to push a bigger gear up hills, but generally you will find that this will tire your legs more quickly. It is also more efficient to stay seated in the saddle, but racers may need to 'jump on the pedals' to accelerate up the climb. All riders may find that occasionally getting out of the saddle may help them get over certain short, steep sections.

If you're climbing under a lot of pressure you may try 'ankling' to try and maximise the force through as much of the pedal stroke as possible (see Tip below).

At the summit, don't change up immediately but keep your cadence high for a few extra revolutions to allow your legs to recover. Then change up and accelerate as the downhill begins. But remember to first change into a smaller gear before changing into the larger chain ring (as explained on p. 34).

TIP

Ankling: by changing the angle of your foot during the pedal stroke you can apply more force to the cranks throughout the whole revolution, providing a smoother, more efficient pedalling stroke that mobilises more of your leg muscles for extra power.

Point your toes slightly up at the top of the stroke (when your foot is at 12 o'clock) and down at the bottom (6 o'clock). You will feel the extra work being done by your calf muscles as you aim to reduce the 'dead spots' at the point where the force changes between the upward and downward strokes.

WEATHER CONDITIONS –
CYCLING IN THE RAIN

If it starts raining, the riding conditions will change dramatically as the road becomes slippery and your tyres and breaking performance also change.

Give yourself extra braking distance and more time to react as you approach junctions or obstacles. The rims get wet in the rain and the first few seconds of applying the brakes serves to clear water off the braking surface of the rim. Give yourself a few extra seconds to dry the rims; you will sense when they are dry enough to give better and more powerful braking. You should also pay attention to changes in the road surface, which may change your tyre grip.

If it's raining before you start your ride you may consider lowering the air pressure in your tyres to give you a little extra grip and control.

When riding in wet conditions:

- Be more careful when cornering.
- Watch out for drain covers, white lines and road markings, which become extremely slippery in the wet.
- Watch out for puddles, which may cover holes or wet leaves in the road. Try to avoid them if possible.
- Watch out for railway crossings, which can become slippery in the wet.
- Remember that motorists will find it harder to see you. Make sure you're wearing a brightly coloured rain jacket, ideally one with reflective strips, and/or a high-visibility vest.

TIP
Braking distances are doubled in the wet!

FACT
Cycling at least twenty miles a week cuts your risk of heart disease in half compared to non-cyclists who take no exercise, according to the British Heart Foundation.

4: RIDING WITH OTHERS

Whether you ride off-road or on-road, you will often be sharing the trail or the road with others. There may be other cyclists, or on highways there will be motorised traffic. Like all road users, you must obey the rules, and you should also be aware of cycling etiquette and some practical techniques that are useful when you're with other cyclists.

RIDING IN A GROUP

There are lots of benefits to riding in company or in a group. You can share your cycling experience with friends or family, facing the challenges of the road together and sharing the events of a ride, whether conquering a new route or hill or simply enjoying the views and scenery. Sometimes you can also talk and chat as you ride, which is not always possible in other sports or activities.

In addition to the camaraderie there are other benefits too: by following the rider in front you can benefit from their slipstream, which reduces airflow resistance and allows you to ride more easily at the same speed, or faster for the same effort! This is known as 'drafting' in North America. Speed for free!

It is an important skill to master and is a huge benefit in racing, but to be able to ride close to the rider in front takes time. First you must build up confidence in your own ability to ride straight. Then, once you're happy with the idea of riding closer to someone else, you must have confidence in their skill. This is best practised with someone you know. You can explain that you're going to practise riding a little closer and they can try to hold a straight line while you improve.

Remember, if you're riding in a group of people you don't know, give them the benefit of the doubt and leave a little more space than normal until you have built up confidence in their ability.

TIP

The closer you follow the back wheel of the rider in front, the more shelter you get from wind resistance. But get too close and a small movement or change in direction due to a gust of wind or a corner may cause you to touch wheels and lose control, or even crash.

TIP
In a group, try to look forward beyond the rider in front, if possible. This will help you to react quicker to obstacles coming up further down the road. Don't stare in a trance at the back wheel of the rider in front!

We'll talk more about the advantages of pace-lines for racers in a moment, but there are a number of other things to think about when riding in a group. These can throw up some other challenges, as well as some advantages. Communication is a key factor.

Warnings: The first rider in the line should point out well in advance any dangers or obstacles on the road, like holes, litter, puddles or glass, either by shouting out or by pointing with an arm and hand to where the danger lies. The riders following should repeat the information, so that by a chain reaction the last rider will know that, for example, there is a hole on the left coming up, despite not having a clear vision in front because it's blocked by the preceding riders. The same procedure should be followed when turning corners or passing cars.

Junctions: When approaching a junction or traffic lights, the first rider should shout 'Stop!' or 'Red light!' to help those further back to react and brake safely. To help the fluidity of the group at junctions it's also helpful to shout 'Clear!' if there are no cars approaching. Even so, every rider must still check for themselves, because a car may appear after the first few riders have passed. In this case the rider should then shout 'Car!', to alert the riders behind that a car is approaching the junction and give them more time to react.

Keeping together: On a group ride, when riders become separated due to junctions or traffic, it is courteous to wait and re-group before continuing. In this way you can keep a check that everyone is present. There have been many occasions when one rider has had a puncture or a mechanical problem and the group has continued without them. This can cause many problems if the lone rider is on unknown roads or does not have all the tools to fix the bike.

SHARING THE PACE

Because one great benefit of riding in a group is the slipstream effect, it also means that the rider in front is working harder than the riders behind. It therefore makes sense for everyone to take their turn at setting the pace. Overall, the group goes faster when everyone shares the workload. This is a key element for racers and is the reason why the big peloton in the Tour de France can sustain much higher speeds than lone riders or smaller groups. However, riders in Sportives, charity rides, training runs, or just leisure rides with friends can all benefit from 'taking turns at the front'.

When the roads and conditions allow, it's good to ride in 'double file', with two riders side by side followed by riders in pairs behind. The leading pair should aim to ride at a fast but sustainable pace, which keeps the whole group moving at a good speed and offers shelter to the group behind.

By riding at a slightly faster pace than you could keep up permanently by yourself, you do work harder for the time you are leading the group. But your reward comes once the next riders take over and you move into their slipstream. This gives you a chance to recover because you can maintain the same pace with less effort than if you were riding alone. In this way, when it's your turn to ride at the front again, you're fully recovered and ready to do another fast turn.

TIP
Keep your turns brief. The bigger the group, the shorter your turns can be.

TIP

On a club or training run you will all take your turn to move right the way through the pace-line. However, if you're a racer in a large competitive group, then try to avoid riding at the back because the 'yo-yo effect' can make it much more tiring and increase the risk of crashes.

If the pace goes up, then riders will generally do progressively shorter turns at the front, otherwise the whole group will slow down as the lead rider starts to get tired. If this happens, there will be a change in pace as the next rider takes the lead and has to accelerate, making it harder for everyone than if the group keeps the same rhythm.

If you feel too tired to take your turn, it's fine to miss out, but you must realise this in advance and stay out of the way of the changes. Otherwise, any confusion caused will be passed down the group in a 'domino effect'.

Try to avoid sudden changes in pace when taking your turn to pull the group. This means looking ahead to avoid sudden braking, because while you can see what is ahead, the riders further back will not have the same reaction time. This can lead to a concertina effect, which could result in riders at the back not being able to stop in time and possibly colliding with those in front of them.

It also takes time for increases in pace to be transferred to the back of the group, particularly after corners and junctions. If the lead riders accelerate too fast, then the riders at the back will probably end up having to sprint to catch up and then having to brake. This 'yo-yo effect' means they waste a lot of energy.

When riding downhill in a group, the front riders should keep pedalling in order to keep the pace as high as possible. If they don't, the riders behind them can experience a 'slingshot' effect from the slipstream and start to overtake the leading riders. This can cause confusion. Alternatively, if the second-placed riders have to brake to deal with this, the flow of the whole group is disrupted.

CHANGING TURNS

Whether riding in single or double file, on- or off-road, ending your turn at the front is much the same. You need to move over to allow the riders behind to come through, and ease off the pace just enough to allow the whole group to pass you. Don't freewheel, but keep a steady pace and then accelerate again a little as you see the back of the line. In this way you can match your speed to that of the group as you take your position, making sure you don't cut across in front of other riders.

If you're riding anti-clockwise on an oval track you would move over to the right, up the banking, to allow others to pass, always checking first that there are no riders outside you and that it's safe to do so. When riding on the road, you move towards the centre of the carriageway, allowing the group to pass on your inside, but before moving out you need to take a quick look behind to check for traffic. Move to the middle of your lane so that you allow just enough room for the group to pass. Don't go too far into the middle so that you're blocking the road and don't stay too close so that the other riders are squeezed into the curb trying to pass you.

TIP

While you're at the back of the group you have a good opportunity to take a drink and recover before moving through the line again.

SIDE WINDS

We've talked about the slipstream benefit of riding in a group and this becomes even more important when it's windy. If the wind changes direction, then changing the way the group lines up can ensure you continue to get the maximum benefit. The following paragraphs relate to countries in which the traffic drives on the left-hand side of the road. 'Right' and 'left' should be reversed for countries where driving on the right is the norm.

As a guide, you should be following directly behind the rider in front when the wind is directly in your face (a head wind) or straight at your back (a tail wind). If the angle begins to change so that it becomes more of a cross-wind, you should move around the wheel of the rider in front to the side with the most shelter. So if the wind is blowing from your left, you should ride just a few centimetres to the right side of the back wheel of the person in front.

If the wind is blowing from the right, the first pair in the group should ride out towards the middle of the road, allowing the following riders to overlap on the left-hand side without having to ride in the gutter at the edge of the road. Common sense should prevail here because there will probably be enough room, depending on the width of the road, for four or five pairs to overlap. The remaining riders will have to follow directly behind each other, but usually the rider in fifth or sixth position will have a lot of slipstream shelter anyway and will not have the same need to maximise the overlap to get protection from the side-wind.

TIP

Watch out for gusting winds from gates or gaps in the hedgerow, and especially from passing lorries, which have a big suction effect. Hold the handlebars a little more firmly as you anticipate gusts of wind.

FACT

Cyclists absorb lower levels of pollutants from traffic fumes than car drivers.

RIDING IN TRAFFIC

As cyclists, we usually have to share the road with motorists, some of whom will be more cycling-aware than others. Riding in groups is great because you are more noticeable, but ride in single file when it's busy. You should respect motorists' rights but always ride confidently – don't allow yourself to be intimidated. Whether alone or in a group, observing these guidelines will make you safer and also help the traffic flow smoothly:

- Anticipate the actions of other road users and be alert to possible hazards, especially at junctions, where motorists may turn across in front of you. Making eye contact establishes they have seen you.
- Always signal your intentions clearly and don't make sudden actions or swerve (if you're overtaking a fellow cyclist, call out if necessary and don't cut in too sharply).
- Make it easy for motorists to see you: wear a high-visibility vest and make sure your lights work.
- Obey the rules; don't be tempted to jump red lights or ride on the pavement.
- Don't underestimate the speed of vehicles and the power of their brakes; don't ride too close behind them.
- Don't ride in the gutter; riding about 75cm from the curb will make you more visible and prevent motorists from squeezing past when there isn't enough room. You will also avoid most of the debris. (Try 'jumping' over unavoidable holes or obstacles, holding the handlebars firmly and straight, with your feet in the 3–9 o'clock position.)
- Do use your eyes and ears. Look about 30–50m ahead so you can react to obstacles and changes in the road surface and listen for car horns, revving engines, squealing brakes and skidding tyres. (I never ride in traffic with music.)

- Don't weave in and out of slow-moving traffic or dodge in and out round parked cars (and beware of doors being opened unexpectedly).
- Change gear well in advance of junctions or traffic lights, to give you more control, and be decisive if you have the right of way – don't dither.
- Stop in the centre of the road at traffic lights to show your presence; don't let motorists try to push you towards the curb.
- Take particular care on the nearside of lorries and buses, especially at junctions; you may well be in a blind spot and as the vehicle turns the corner it may cut across your path.
- Don't shout abuse or make obscene signs at drivers, even if they're in the wrong. If you do encounter deliberately inconsiderate or dangerous drivers, try memorising their number plate and reporting them to the police.
- As a last resort to try and avoid an accident, shout! This may be the split second that alerts the driver to your presence and prevents an accident.

5:LOOKING AFTER YOUR BIKE

Before we look at ways to get you into top shape, we must look at one more important bike basic – maintenance. It's easy to focus on getting ourselves fitter to achieve our cycling aims, but our machines also need to be fit to ride. A well-maintained bike is not only safer but will ride better and faster. Bikes are very efficient machines and regular checks mean you can deal with minor problems and repairs as soon as you notice them. If you keep your cycle in good working order you should be able to enjoy more time riding it rather than fixing it!

WEEKLY WASH

If you ride daily, it's worth cleaning your bike once a week to keep the equipment clean and in good running order; this will also stop components wearing out and make your bike last longer. Unless your bike is particularly dirty, all you need is a bucket of warm water with washing-up liquid and a sponge or soft rag.

- Start by cleaning the frame, saddle, seat post, handlebars and stem. Check for any cracks or broken paint which could indicate damage to the frame.
- Take the front wheel out and clean inside the crown of the forks and the front brake calliper.
- Take the back wheel out and clean inside the rear triangle and the rear brake calliper.
- With the wheels out, clean the rims, spokes and hubs. You may need to use a degreaser. This will allow you to break down the greasy residues from lubrication that has picked up dirt. There are many specialist bike degreasers available from your bike shop or online, including ecological biodegradable products. Having first used these to displace the grime you can then finish off the job with soapy water to rinse it away.

- Use a toothbrush or special brush to clean between the teeth of the sprockets on your rear wheel cassette. Do the same with the rear and front derailleur, and then the chain and chain rings.

There is no need to dry your bike; if there are still soapsuds, rinse the bike with clean water and the chemicals in the washing-up liquid should make it shine!

If your chain is very dirty you can remove it and soak it in paraffin for a few hours. Clean it with a stiff brush or wire brush to remove all the dirt and then put it back on the bike. You could also use a special chain-cleaning bath which clips over the chain. After filling it with degreaser, turn the pedals backwards, moving the chain through until it's clean.

TIP
Be careful not to let drops of oil or lubricant
fall onto the rims or onto the brake blocks.

LUBRICATION

The final stage after washing is to lubricate your bike to protect
it from rust and corrosion, and to reduce any friction on the
moving parts. Gone are the days when riders used multi-
purpose oil on the moving parts of their bikes. These days there
is an array of products designed specifically to cope with the
technical requirements of modern bikes. From organic eco-
lubes to hi-tech chemicals containing specialised substances
such as Teflon, you can choose the product which best suits
you and your type of cycling. Some lubricants are dry, and
ideally suited to road riding in good conditions. Wet lubes are

more suitable if you ride a lot in the rain or in muddy
conditions.

Whatever type you use, before you apply the lubricant, wipe
the chain to remove any excess water and then lubricate the
chain, the rear and front gear derailleur, the front and rear hubs
(including the freewheel), the brake callipers, and any cables
that are exposed or where they go in or out of the cable
casings. Grease the pedal axles and also grease any moving
parts on your cleats. Apply some grease to bolts to stop them
going rusty too.

QUICK CHECKS

After cleaning and lubricating your bike the next step is to make a few quick checks.

TYRES

Check your tyres for cuts and wear of the tread. Remove any glass or stones that may be embedded in the tyre. If you see any deep cuts or bald patches, it's time to change the tyre.

WHEELS

- First spin the wheel to see if it's running 'true'. To check your wheel is true use a fixed reference point like the brake block and watch whether the rim stays at a constant distance for the whole revolution or if it deflects back and forth.
- Check the tension of your spokes. Any loose or broken spokes mean that your wheel is not balanced, and even if it's still running 'true', hitting one bump or pot-hole when you're out riding could slightly buckle your wheel. Remember that the spokes on the freewheel (gear) side of the rear wheel will be slightly tighter than those attaching to the other side of the hub.

If your wheel is well out of true you may wish to take it to your local bike shop, where an experienced mechanic or wheel builder with a wheel truing jig can return it to perfect shape. This may not be possible or you may just want to have a go at it yourself. If you don't have your own jig, then use the frame of your bike (as described in the text) to gauge how true the wheel is.

You can adjust the tension of spokes by using a spoke key to tighten or loosen the nipple. To replace damaged spokes you need to remove the tyre and inner tube, and also the rim tape. You can then unscrew the nipple with a screwdriver and take the spoke out of its hole in the flange of the hub. To insert a spoke, follow the procedure in reverse, remembering to lace it the same way between the other spokes if they are crossed over.

- Check for any lateral movement in the wheel. If it does move, the wheel bearings are probably loose.

BRAKES

- Check that your brake blocks are all making full contact with the rim. They should not be set up too low, so that they are only half touching the braking surface, or too high, in case they touch and go through the side wall of your tyre.
- Check the wear of your brake pads.
- Check that your brake calliper is central, so that when you apply the brakes both brake pads touch the rim at the same time.

TIP

When replacing brake blocks take care to buy the correct type; the majority are made from rubber but there are also cork pads for carbon rims.

It's possible that one set of brake blocks will wear out quicker than the other, so check that your brakes all come on at the same time. To do this, apply both brakes; the contact point should occur at the same position for both brake levers. If one set comes on sooner, you will give brake unevenly. To correct this, adjust the cable by turning the adjuster on the brake calliper (road bikes) or on the brake lever (mountain bikes).

GEARS

- Check that the gears work properly, making the correct selection and running smoothly in each gear. Do this by going through the gears while turning the pedals with the rear wheel off the ground.
- Test extreme changes, like big ring to small ring in large and small sprockets. If adjustments need to be made, there are positioning screws on the front changer and rear mechanism, as well as cable adjusters to ensure the optimum set-up.
- Check for play in the rear mechanism and jockey wheels.

CHAIN

Try lifting the chain up off the big ring; if you can see the tooth of the chain ring, it's time to replace the chain.

If you replace your chain, it's also worth checking the condition of your sprockets. These will also wear out, though much more slowly than your chain. If you're not sure about the sprockets, you can get them checked, or you may find out the hard way if your gears start to 'jump' when you're cycling. This happens because the new chain is not meshing properly with the sprocket teeth and you need to replace the sprockets.

BOTTOM BRACKET AND CHAINSET

- Check for play in the bottom bracket; any sideways movement means a loss of pedalling power so it may need adjusting or replacing.
- Check the cranks and the pedals; if they are bent, they need replacing.
- Any grinding, clicking or squeaking could mean loose or worn parts, so check the tightness of the chain ring bolts and bottom bracket. Check that everything is running freely by taking the chain off and then spinning the pedals around with no chain. They should spin freely in silence; if they don't spin, the bottom bracket is tight and needs fixing or replacing.

HEAD SET AND HANDLEBARS

- Check the tightness of your handlebars by holding the front wheel between your knees and trying to turn the handlebars.
- Check the headset by applying the front brake firmly and trying to rock the bike backwards and forwards. If there is some rocking and movement, you need to tighten the headset.

TIP

To adjust a threadless headset, first loosen the side bolts then make the adjustment with the top bolt. Make sure you don't tighten it too much so that the steering is 'sticky'. If you can't get the right set-up, take it to be checked at a bike shop.

BOLTS

Check that all bolts are secure. Go methodically through the bike, checking that gear derailleurs, brake callipers and cables are all tight. Check the seat clamp, handlebar stem, headset, bottom bracket, chain ring bolts, pedals and bottle-cage bolts. Check your brake and gear levers are also tight.

TIP

If you replace some equipment or cables, check the tightness of the bolts after a couple of rides to make sure they are not coming loose.

FACT

Approximately one hundred bikes can be produced from the materials used to produce a single motor vehicle.

TIP
If you cannot find a puncture in
the inner tube, check the valve,
which may be leaking air.

PUNCTURES

Major improvements in tyre technology mean that punctures are nowhere near as frequent as they once were. However, you're unlikely to escape this most common bicycle mishap completely. Unless you have tubeless tyres, a puncture means you'll have to repair or replace the inner tube.

- Remove the wheel, and look for signs of the thorn, nail, glass or other cause of the puncture on the outside of the tyre. If you can see it, remove it.
- If any air remains in the inner tube let it all out, and then slide two tyre levers a little distance apart underneath the tyre. Be very careful not to 'pinch' the inner tube as this may cause an additional hole.
- Lever the tyre over the rim, and if your tyre levers have hooks, hook them to the spokes below.
- Using a third tyre lever, or by keeping one tyre lever in place, move round the tyre, easing it off the rim. As you get further round, the tyre will become looser and you may be able to use your fingers to take the beading of one side of the tyre off the rim. There is no need to remove the whole tyre at this stage.
- Keeping the valve in the rim, remove the inner tube until only the valve is left in the wheel. Pump up the inner tube and listen for a hissing of air coming out of the inner tube.
- If you can locate the hole, match the position in the inner tube with the position in the tyre and check it for any offending sharp objects. Even if you find the culprit, it's worth using your fingers or a rag to wipe the whole of the inside of the tyre to make sure it's debris free.
- If you cannot find the puncture by looking and listening, you may need to remove the inner tube completely and fill a bowl or sink with water. Check the inner tube by submerging it under water to look for air bubbles escaping from the hole.
- You can either use a puncture repair kit to patch the hole, or alternatively replace the whole inner tube.
- To put the inner tube back on the rim, first place the valve through the rim, and pump in a little air, just enough so you can put it back into place easily.
- Feed the inner tube under the tyre so that it's sitting inside all the way round.
- Push the beading of the tyre over the rim with your thumbs to begin with, and then if necessary with the tyre levers, being careful not to pinch the inner tube between the tyre lever and the tyre.
- Replace the wheel into the frame or forks and check the beading is sitting evenly on the rim by spinning the tyre round.
- Now you can pump up the tyre, before making a final check that the tyre is still sitting properly on the rim after inflating.

TIP
Metal tyre levers should only be
used on steel rims. Plastic levers
can be used on all types of rims.

TOOLED UP

It's important to be prepared to deal with punctures or any mechanical problems that may occur when you're out riding. You don't know where it may happen; if you're somewhere isolated, then having some basic tools will help you fix the problem, or at least help you fix it well enough to either get you back home or to the nearest bike shop!

There is obviously a line to be drawn between having all eventualities covered and the inconvenience of carrying more than is strictly necessary. There are, however, some basics you should always have with you.

PUMPS

Pumps can fit onto the frame, or onto brackets, or there are mini-pumps which easily fit into your back pocket. Another alternative is carbon dioxide canisters. These can inflate inner tubes in seconds, but normally will only be of use for one puncture. You therefore have to carry several or run the risk of being stuck if you have more than one flat tyre on a ride. There are some hybrid canister casings that double up as basic pumps for emergencies.

TIP

Bike valves come in two types – long thin 'Presta' valves, or wider car-style 'Schraeder' valves. Make sure your pump or canister has the correct adapter for the type on your bike.

In addition to a pump you will need either a puncture repair kit or spare inner tubes. One or two can fit into a small bag under your saddle, along with three tyre levers and a multi-tool.

FACT

The cost of buying a bike is approximately 1 per cent of the cost of buying a car.

MULTI-TOOLS

These are fantastic for combining allen keys, screwdrivers, possibly a chain link extractor and even tyre levers or spoke keys into one multi-functional tool. It means that you can deal with most mechanical problems out on the road and you don't have lots of tools jingling about while you're riding.

TIP

Wrap your tools and tyre levers in a rag or an old sock to stop them making a noise while you ride. It also stops sharp ends piercing your saddle bag.

TOOLBOX

In your home or garage it's worth having a bigger selection of tools for repairs.

- Track pump: This type of pump stands on the floor and is operated by two hands, and usually has a gauge. It's easier to use than a hand pump and you can regulate the exact tyre pressure.
- Spanners
- Allen keys
- Screwdrivers
- Chain link extractor
- Bottom bracket tools/extractor
- Headset tools
- Spoke key
- Pliers
- Puncture repair kit
- Insulation tape

It is also good to keep some spares in stock for unplanned repairs:
- Inner tubes, rim tapes and tyres
- Gear and brake cables
- Cable casings/outers
- Nuts and bolts
- Light bulbs or batteries for lights
- Spokes and nipples

6:ADDITIONAL EQUIPMENT

We've already looked at what type of bike to buy, and some of the clothing that can improve your cycling experience and performance. There are, though, a few other options to consider before you're completely set up – items such as locks for security, lights for safety and computers to track your progress.

LOCKS

Sadly many bikes are stolen, often from garages and sheds. Always make sure that your bike is secure, even at home. Cycle tourists and commuters, or any riders who leave their bikes unattended in public places, have slightly different problems. You will need to find a lock that is suitable for your needs and the value of your bike, but you also have to think about how you will carry it with you. If you're leaving your bike for short lengths of time, or within sight, a lightweight lock will probably be sufficient, but if you have to leave it for a long time, or it's particularly valuable, a sturdier, heavy lock would be better.

Remember when leaving your bike to take all removable items such as lights with you, and if you have a quick-release saddle or wheels, wrap the lock through these as well as through the closed part of the frame.

TIP

Make sure your bike is properly insured. Cycle theft is an increasing problem, especially in big cities, and even the highest-calibre locks may not always protect your bike from the determined thief.

BEING SEEN

It is essential to be seen by other road users, especially if you have to ride in low light levels or darkness. You can do this by making sure you wear bright clothes, and/or a high-visibility vest. Reflectors really help too. Your bike may already have reflectors, including those on pedals and wheels, but you can also buy reflective tape and put reflective strips down your forks or seat stays, or on the back of a mudguard. You can also get reflective strips on clothes, helmets or bags.

LIGHTS

For more visibility, and also to allow you to see where you're going in the dark, you will need lights. Riding in the dark without lights is an offence.

LED lights have become increasingly popular as they have become brighter. They are efficient long-lasting lights that can be either white or red. They can be used in steady or flashing modes, are low maintenance, don't require much battery power, and are relatively cheap. If you want a more powerful beam for seeing on unlit roads, or even for off-road cycling, then you can also buy powerful halogen beam lamps. These can be expensive, and though they run off rechargeable battery packs, these may be large and have short burn times.

You need to weigh up your budget and your requirements before selecting the most appropriate lightning, but remember that not only do you need to see and be seen, you also have to comply with the law in your country.

Other lighting options you may consider include Pedalites. These are special pedals with flashing lights that require no batteries at all. They are powered by the motion of pedalling, but continue to shine for several minutes after you have stopped. This is a similar idea to front or rear dynamo lights, which run off a small generator turned by your moving tyre. But this does add extra resistance to your riding!

TIP

Some dynamos don't contain a capacitor to keep your lights on when the wheel isn't turning. If this is the case, remember that if you're stationary, as at traffic lights, you will have no lights, so a back-up reflector or simple LED light will help.

Particularly useful for off-road riding in the dark are small lights which can attach to your helmet. These make sure that the beam is thrown in the direction you're looking.

HOW FAR, HOW FAST?

If you want to know how far you've ridden (or how much further it is to your destination!) and how fast you're riding you need a bike computer. These vary from very cheap basic units to expensive highly sophisticated instruments that can deliver all the information you could possibly want. Small, lightweight and battery powered, they give you immediate information while you're riding at the touch of the button. Basic information includes speed and distance, while the more advanced models also measure cadence, power, altitude and heart rate. These data can be very valuable in improving your fitness and we'll talk more about that later.

KEEPING CLEAN

If you're commuting throughout the year, or doing a lot of riding in the rainy, winter months, mudguards will really help protect you from the spray of water from the road. Some frames have mudguard eyes where you can use nuts and bolts to secure the supports to the frame. But there are other possibilities for bikes without these brazed-on attachments.

Fixed front/rear: These are good long-term solutions and come in different lengths to give you almost full protection.
Removable: These come in a variety of styles and clip onto your seat post for rear wheel protection, or onto your down tube to protect you from spray or mud from the front. These are great for the odd rainy day and are easily removed if you need to transport your bike. They are also useful on mountain bikes to protect you from the mud.

SADDLE BAGS, PANNIERS AND CARRIERS

To carry the basic tools a saddle bag is ideal. However, if you will be carrying a change of clothes or bulky items, or need to take supplies for a touring trip, panniers fitted onto a carrier are ideal. The carrier attaches to mudguard eyes near the drop-outs and the panniers can be clipped or tied onto your carrier.

TIP

Take some 'bungees' or spare toe-straps with you to help fix your pannier or bag in place; you don't want it to be moving or rocking around while you're cycling.

BIKE RACKS

If you're transporting your bike there are a variety of bike racks available for your car. Roof racks enable you to transport the bikes and still have access to your boot but they add to the car's air resistance.

Rear-mounted racks are more economical for your car's fuel consumption but some models don't allow you to open the boot while the rack is mounted. It's best to get specialist advice, depending on your car and how many bikes you plan to transport.

PART TWO

BODY BASICS

We've looked at the bike, at the gadgets and gizmos to make it look, feel and ride better, and at the basic skills required to handle it comfortably and confidently. Cycling, however, is a combination of (wo)man and machine, so never overlook the importance of the rider.

In this section you will find training plans suitable for different levels of ability as well as how to get your body in shape for successful riding, including strength and flexibility training and nutritional advice.

1: FIT TO RIDE

If your skill and fitness levels don't match your aims, then you can expect to have an unsuccessful and frustrating time. A beautiful bike will soon lose its appeal on social rides if you struggle to keep up; an expensive bike is no guarantee of completing a Sportive if you haven't invested in your body; and all the latest technology won't win you races unless you fine tune the engine that makes it go. It's vital, therefore, that you get your body into the right shape to match your ambitions, and that you maintain it with an appropriate routine. This should include a 'training schedule', off-bike care such as stretching, good nutrition and a positive attitude.

The good news is that many people find getting fitter makes them healthier and happier, and motivates them to improve or increase their fitness still further. The key, though, is to push yourself enough to make improvements, but not so much that your body can't cope or you no longer enjoy it. Your reward from cycling might be winning races, achieving challenging goals, or just the thrill of cruising through the countryside, but if it stops giving you that sense of achievement and fun, then you need to take a look at your approach.

FACT

A moderate commute of half an hour each way will burn 8 calories a minute, or the equivalent of 11kg of fat in a year.

TRAINING DIARIES

As you start to build up your cycling, by going out on the bike more frequently or by increasing the distance you ride, you may find it both motivational and useful to start keeping a journal or training diary. The big benefit of keeping a diary specifically monitoring your cycling activities is to provide a factual account of the different elements of your riding. This will be a useful tool in helping you reach the goals and targets you have set yourself, give you clues on how to work on any of your weaknesses and help you see patterns in what riding worked best for you in the past.

There are many different ways to keep a training diary, and many different factors you may wish to include. Noting the length of rides, the time they took and the terrain you covered would be an ideal starting point. You could also include your feelings and perceptions. Did you feel rough at the start but finish strongly? Did you find your climbing to be strong but riding on the flat a little hard going? Were you motivated to get out on your bike or were you feeling tired and sore from a lot of riding the day before? Noting your feelings will help you reflect on your riding and also potentially help you work out whether something happened in the rides or days before which caused this good or bad feeling. Writing honestly about your ride and anything else relevant to your cycling will help you keep track of your progress as you improve.

If you're using a heart rate monitor (see p. 72), you may want to think about getting computer software that allows you to download your training information directly. You can then analyse your riding performance in great detail and see exactly what zones you're working most in.

Remember, everyone is different, so there is no right or wrong information to put in your diary; it is personal to you and you should use this as a way to get the most out of your cycling.

A diary is also a good way of holding yourself to account if you're following a training plan. If you have a diary with enough space to set out what rides you aim to do at the top, and what you actually do at the bottom, you'll soon see whether or not you're taking the right steps towards your goals.

TRAINING DIARY TIPS

Keep it factual
Be honest
Review regularly
Use the feedback!

Wednesday 12 March

3 a.m.

6 a.m.   8 hours sleep, slightly tired this morning and legs
feel stiff. Weather good 19°, some sun, slight wind.

9 a.m.   Rode 'Hilly Circuit One'. Sluggish to start but felt good after the
first half hour. Total time 2 hours 17 minutes 16 secs, only 1
minute forty outside my best time! Maximum heart rate on final
climb 187. Weight 62kg.

12 p.m.

3 p.m.

Afternoon: Rest

6 p.m.

9 p.m.   Feeling a bit 'achey'. Early night.

TRAINING PLANS

If you're a complete novice, or returning to cycling after a long period of non-fitness, then make sure you're healthy enough to begin increasing the amount of exercise that you're going to do. If you're in any doubt, consult a medical adviser first and possibly have an appropriate health check before following any of the plans in this book.

Whether you're following a serious training schedule, or just gradually increasing the distance and pace you ride at, the processes involved in becoming a fitter, stronger and faster rider are the same. Imagine you can ride a certain distance comfortably. Now consider what happens if you ride that little bit further, so that it becomes a bit of a challenge to complete the ride. The automatic response of your body as it recovers from the effort is to rebuild itself that little bit stronger to cope with a similar demand in the future. The same process applies if you try to ride faster than you're used to, or try to cycle up steeper hills.

There are two elements to the training process – the stress and the recovery – and both are vitally important. There must be enough stress to encourage the body's adaptive processes, but not too much to cause serious damage. The recovery is the time when the transformation takes place, so don't skip it or you risk having the opposite effect to the desired improvement.

As long as you're sensible, a casual approach will give certain benefits if you're starting from a low level of fitness and your ultimate goals are not set very high. At the other end of the scale, a dedicated competitive cyclist seeking to maximise possible gains needs a carefully prepared plan to keep improving. It's not just racers, however, who can benefit from a well-thought-out structured schedule. By following a sensible but challenging timetable even novices should find they make progress quickly and safely.

Think of a training plan as a route map – how to get from A to B. 'A' is your current level of fitness and 'B' is where your fitness levels should be, having completed the trip. Each plan will only be a short journey on the way to a longer-term destination. So in order to work out this 'route', you need to know where you're heading: work out some goals and then devise a sensible step-by-step programme for achieving that target within the desired period. To begin with, it may just be something simple like being able to ride the bike every day, or perhaps being able to complete a ride of a certain distance or duration. For fitter riders, it will be about achieving peak performance for certain targeted events.

Any training plan needs to be achievable within the context of work and social or family commitments, providing just enough of a challenge to keep you motivated and improve your riding. The fitter you get, the more precisely you can tailor your plan to particular performance elements. Remember – a plan is just a plan. Sometimes circumstances may make you miss or change certain sessions, but if this happens frequently, then you need to re-think the schedules you're setting yourself, and quite possibly the targets you're aiming for too.

Many people tend to have more time at the weekends to enjoy longer rides, and this tends to be when events such as Sportives and races take place. But if you have other commitments on Saturdays and Sundays, or have time off on weekdays, you can easily make adjustments to plans that specify greater longer sessions at weekends. If your time is limited, consider combining certain training rides with commuting to work, if that's possible (see chapter 10). Other alternatives, which may help you fit training elements into your daily life, include split sessions, or perhaps indoor riding on rollers or a 'turbo-trainer'.

You must have the discipline to stick with your plan if you want to reach your targets, but you must also be sensible and listen to your body. If you really feel that you're not up to a scheduled ride because you haven't recovered from a previous session, because you're tired, or because you're ill, then don't worry about skipping it. In the long run it will do you far more good to take a sensible approach rather than run your body down and make things worse. In the case of illness you should wait until you're fully recovered before resuming your training plan, and in the event of a lengthy lay-off, don't try to continue at the level you were at before your illness. You will need to build up to it again.

On the other hand, if you have to miss a particular session because of an unforeseen commitment, you may easily be able to reschedule it. For instance, if you run out of time for a Tuesday session and have an easy or rest day scheduled for Wednesday, then simply slot the session in on the Wednesday, unless it would compromise the plan for Thursday.

A turbo-trainer is usually an A-frame construction to which you attach the rear wheel of your bike. The tyre presses against a roller, which provides resistance to allow you to ride your normal bike in a static location. Turbo-trainers can be very useful if you have limited time, especially in winter when bad weather or lack of daylight restricts the amount of time you can spend on roads or trails.

The cheapest models use air resistance, while those that use fluid will be quieter. Alternatively, an electro-magnetic system allows you to have a handlebar control to increase or reduce resistance, and the most expensive systems can be connected to a computer to provide the added stimulus of computer-generated courses or even video simulations. This highlights one of the main drawbacks of the turbo-trainer – they can be very boring. They are best kept for short rides, but can be very useful for highly controlled higher-intensity sessions, such as 'interval training' (see p. 73).

Remember, if you're riding indoors with no wind to cool you, you will get very hot, so drink plenty of liquid, protect any items that may get showered in sweat, and if possible, set up a fan to help with cooling.

GETTING REGULAR: THE FOUR-HOUR PLAN

This first plan is designed to go from little or no cycling to riding regularly. The aim is to get to four hours cycling a week and give a basic level of fitness to build on. Starting with three short rides a week, it gradually builds up the duration and adds in a fourth day during the second half of the plan. Like the other plans in this book, it's based on an eight-week period – a seven-week training block followed by an easier week to ensure adequate recovery and avoid over-training. After an active rest week you should feel refreshed and ready for another seven-week block, building on the previous plan. The final week also includes a test to enable you to judge your progress. This could simply be riding your favourite route to see how quickly you can do it, or something more specific, aimed at identifying measurable fitness values to work out training zones.

So how hard do you ride? Since the aim of this first plan is simply to get you riding regularly and provide a base for those with limited experience, just go out and ride at a steady pace. You need to put in a little effort, but you shouldn't be totally exhausted at the end. As a guide, if you're riding with someone else you should be able to talk to them, but find you need to pause frequently to breathe.

In later plans there will be more variety of pacing across the week and throughout a session, so you need to know how to judge your effort. Sometimes you will need to ride easily, often you will ride steadily; there will be times when you will work hard, and others when you will go very hard or flat out. Descriptions like that are based on personal perceptions. Even with all the scientific methods

GETTING REGULAR – THE 4-HOUR PLAN

WEEK	Mon	Tues	Weds	Thurs	Fri	Sat	Sun
1	Day off	35 mins green	Day off	35 mins green	Day off	45 mins green	Rest or other exercise
2	Day off	40 mins green	Day off	40 mins green	Day off	50 mins green	Rest or other exercise
3	Day off	45 mins green	Day off	45 mins green	Day off	55 mins green	Rest or other exercise
4	Day off	50 mins green	Day off	50 mins green	Day off	60 mins green	Rest or other exercise
5	Day off	50 mins green	Day off	50 mins green	Day off	60 mins green	30 mins green
6	Day off	55 mins green	Day off	55 mins green	Day off	70 mins green	35 mins green
7	Day off	60 mins green	Day off	60 mins green	Day off	75 mins green	45 mins green
8	Day off	30 mins green	Day off	30 mins green	Day off	Test	Rest

Why is the plan eight weeks long? It is thought that it takes six to eight weeks for the body to respond to training. The plan provides seven weeks of steady progression followed by one recovery week. You then need to change your training schedule to make further improvements. If you keep repeating the same schedule, then you won't see any change.

available today some experienced cyclists still prefer to train on 'feel', and are very adept at judging their effort surprisingly accurately.

Going back to the analogy of holding a conversation, riding easily should allow you to chat freely. If you're working hard, you should still be able to speak, but you'll need to take several gulps of air during sentences, and once it gets to the very hard stage you'll be down to noises rather than words! In these plans, the levels from easy to flat out are divided into five zones: blue, green, yellow, amber and red (see p. 73).

MEASURING YOUR HEART RATE

For many years, and until surprisingly recently, even the most successful cyclists based their training on the old fashioned notion of 'getting the miles in'. They just went out and rode for hour after hour, using the same traditional routines that had been accepted for years. Pioneers like 1977 World Road Race Champion Francesco Moser and 1992 Olympic Pursuit Champion Chris Boardman brought a more scientific approach to cycling, and there have been many advances in our understanding of exercise physiology over the last few decades, not to mention ways to monitor performance.

The first bicycle computer was introduced in the 1980s, making it easy for riders to measure speed and distance travelled. During the 1990s heart rate monitors became commonplace, providing valuable training feedback. These were followed by power meters, delivering ever more accurate tools to track performance. For a serious cyclist, the power meter is the most reliable method of monitoring progress, but these can still be expensive. Heart rate monitors cost less and are often combined with other cycle computer functions.

Heart rate is the number of beats your heart makes per minute. At rest this may be 60–80 beats per minute (bpm), but this is highly individual and some highly trained cyclists may have resting heart rates as low as 30bpm. At the other end of the scale, when working at maximum effort your heart rate may rise above 200bpm. A basic generic formula for working out expected maximum heart rates is to deduct your age from 220 (e.g. for a 25–year-old the expected maximum would be 220 – 25 = 195), but this varies widely, and you should try to get an accurately measured value.

Early use of heart rates to determine exercise level simply recommended various percentages of that maximum. A more tailored method is to base it on your heart rate reserve. If your resting heart rate is 50 and your maximum 200, then your heart rate reserve is 150. Therefore exercising at 70 per cent your heart rate would be:

150 x 70% = 105 + 50 = 155

There is, however, an even more useful value – threshold. Simply put, anaerobic threshold is where things get really tough! Also referred to as the lactate threshold, it's the point at which oxygen cannot reach the muscles fast enough, lactate accumulates, and performance suffers. Basing your training on percentages of threshold is better than using heart rate alone, but how do you find out what it is? If you're lucky enough to have access to a sports scientist, accurate measurements can be made from repeated blood samples taken as you gradually increase your effort on a laboratory bike.

Such accurate measurements are not possible for many riders, so instead we can use functional threshold – the maximum level you can sustain for an hour. If you have a bike or a turbo-trainer that will measure power output, then your functional threshold can be related to that; alternatively it can be linked to heart rate. Functional threshold is your own personal fitness indicator. As you get fitter it will rise; similarly, improve your functional threshold and you'll improve your performance at lower intensities too.

The simplest way to determine the effort you can sustain for an hour is to ride as hard as you can for one hour, and then note your average heart rate or power output for the ride. These are your figures for functional threshold. Working this out may not be as easy as it sounds if you don't have that much experience. If you're not ready for the whole hour, just ride for half an hour at a pace you can just maintain for the whole 30 minutes. Use 95 per cent of your recorded average heart rate or power output as your functional threshold. Test yourself at the end of the final active recovery week of each training block so that you can then adjust your training levels to take account of improvements in your fitness.

TIP

When doing either of these tests, make sure you warm up with ten minutes of gentle riding first, and then cool down by continuing to spin an easy gear for at least five minutes afterwards.

There is also a less accurate measure that you can use as a rough starting point if you're not yet fit enough for the test. Like calculating your maximum heart rate by subtracting your age from 220, it can be some way from the correct value, but it will at least provide you with a figure to use until you're ready for the test. Take 80 per cent of your age from 214 if you're male, or 90 per cent of your age from 209 if you're female. Reduce the figure by a further 15 per cent to give you an approximate functional threshold heart rate. For example, for a 30-year-old woman the calculation would be:

30 x 0.9 = 27
209 – 27 = 182
182 x 0.85 = 155

Whichever method you use for identifying these training bands, the key is that as you improve the zones stay the same. No matter how much fitter you become, you can use the same calculations, and it's a great reward to find you can rider faster, for longer, for the same 'effort'.

BLUE RIDES: These rides should be done at a pace where you're just enjoying riding and hardly aware of the 'exercise factor'. They are for **social** rides, **recovery** rides, or **warming up/cooling down** from other sessions.
- Heart rate less than 60 per cent of your maximum heart rate and 69–83 per cent of your functional threshold.
- Functional threshold power 56–75 per cent.

GREEN RIDES: Much of your training will be done at a pace where you start noticing the effort and you need to takes breaths between sentences! It is aimed at improving your **endurance base**.
- Heart rate 60–75 per cent of your maximum and 84–94 per cent of your functional threshold.
- Functional threshold power 76–90 per cent.

YELLOW RIDES: Conversation is severely restricted now as you start to put in much harder work for shorter periods at **effort**.

- Heart rate 75–89 per cent of maximum and 95–105 per cent of your functional threshold.
- Functional threshold power 91–105 per cent.

AMBER RIDES: These are short **high-intensity** efforts measured in minutes and you'll find it hard to say more than the odd word.
- Heart rate 89–94 per cent of maximum and greater than 106 per cent of your functional threshold.
- Functional threshold power 106–120 per cent.

RED RIDES: Talking is out of the question for these very hard, short, intense **interval** bursts. They will last seconds, or just a few minutes within longer sessions.
- Heart rate at least 90 per cent of maximum and greater than 106 per cent of your functional threshold heart rate.
- Functional threshold power at least 121 per cent.

GETTING UP TO SPEED AND IMPROVING ENDURANCE

The next plan takes you from riding around four hours a week to seven hours. It also starts to introduce slightly higher intensities as part of more structured sessions, rather than just going out and riding steadily. It includes one day off completely and a couple of rest days, which may be used as days off or opportunities to do other exercise, such as yoga or swimming (see chapter 8).

Sessions with higher intensities include warming-up and cooling-down periods, and easy (blue) periods in between 'intervals'. This plan gradually increases both the quantity and quality of your training, so make sure you don't overdo things. If you find you're unable to complete the sessions, or are constantly tired, then scale back the training appropriately. Once again, in week 8 take a rest and then take a test! You're sure to find some improvements after all your hard work.

Having built up to seven hours riding a week, you may find that's all you have time for, or all you wish to do. In which case, continue on a similar pattern, bearing in mind the basics of your training plan. You still need to include longer blue/green rides to maintain an endurance base, but you can also include a variety of higher-quality sessions. Incorporate yellow rides of 10–20 minutes, amber rides of 2–5 minutes, and red bursts varying from 10 seconds to 2 minutes (see page 76 for this plan). Remember to build in adequate recovery time between intervals within individual training rides, and rest days after harder sessions. Incorporating complementary exercises on rest days can help to keep you fresh mentally and physically, but make sure you listen to what your body is telling you.

WEEK	Mon	Tues	Weds	Thurs	Fri	Sat	Sun
1	Day off	30 mins 5 blue 20 yellow 5 blue	Rest	60 mins 10 blue 45 yellow 5 blue	60 mins green	Rest	90 mins green
2	Day off	40 mins 5 blue 30 yellow 5 blue	Rest	60 mins 10 blue 45 yellow 5 blue	60 mins green	Rest	105 mins green
3	Day off	50 mins 10 blue 35 yellow 5 blue	Rest	60 mins 10 blue 45 yellow 5 blue	60 mins 20 blue 2 amber 3 blue 20 green 15 blue	Rest	2 hours green
4	Day off	60 mins 10 blue 45 yellow 5 blue	Rest	60 mins 10 blue 45 yellow 5 blue	60 mins 20 blue 2 amber 3 blue 2 amber 3 blue 20 green 10 blue	Rest	150 mins green
5	Day off	70 mins 10 blue 55 yellow 5 blue	Rest	60 mins 10 blue 45 yellow 5 blue	60 mins green	Rest	3 hours green
6	Day off	80 mins 10 blue 65 yellow 5 blue	Rest	60 mins 10 blue 45 yellow 5 blue	60 mins 20 blue 2 amber 3 blue 25 green 10 blue	Rest	210 mins green
7	Day off	60 mins 10 blue 45 yellow 5 blue	Rest	60 mins 10 blue 45 yellow 5 blue	60 mins 20 blue 2 amber 3 blue 2 amber 3 blue 20 green 10 blue	Rest	4 hours green
8	Day off	60 mins 5 blue 20 amber 5 blue	Day off	60 mins 10 blue 45 yellow 5 blue	Day off	Test	Rest

IMPROVING ENDURANCE AND SPEED – THE 7-HOUR PLAN

WEEK	Mon	Tues	Weds	Thurs	Fri	Sat	Sun
1	Day off	90 mins 20 blue 10 yellow 10 blue 10 yellow 10 blue 10 yellow 20 blue	Rest	60 mins green	60 mins 20 blue 5 x (3 amber + 2 blue) 15 blue	Rest	210 mins green
2	Day off	90 mins 20 blue 10 yellow 10 blue 10 yellow 10 blue 10 yellow 20 blue	Rest	60 mins green	60 mins 15 blue 10 x (2 amber + 1blue) 15 blue	Rest	210 mins green Including 1 x (15 yellow +10 blue)
3	Day off	90 mins 30 blue 10 yellow 5 blue 10 yellow 5 blue 10 yellow 20 blue	Rest	60 mins green	60 mins 20 blue 5 x (15 secs red + 45 secs blue) 15 blue 5 x (15 secs red + 45 secs blue) 15 blue	Rest	210 mins green Including 2 x (15 yellow +10 blue)
4	Day off	90 mins 30 blue 10 yellow 5 blue 10 yellow 5 blue 10 yellow 20 blue	Rest	60 mins green	60 mins 25 blue 5 x (30 secs red + 90 secs blue) 25 blue	Rest	210 mins green
5	Day off	90 mins 30 blue 15 yellow 10 blue 15 yellow 20 blue	Rest	60 mins green	60 mins 20 blue 5 x (3 amber +2 blue) 15 blue	Rest	210 mins green Including 2 x (15 yellow +10 blue)
6	Day off	90 mins 30 blue 15 yellow 10 blue 15 yellow 20 blue	Rest	60 mins green	60 mins 15 blue 10 x (2 amber + 1 blue) 15 blue	Rest	210 mins green Including 3 x (15 yellow + 10 blue)
7	Day off	90 mins 30 blue 15 yellow 10 blue 15 yellow 20 blue	Rest	90 mins green	60 mins 20 blue 10 x (1 red + 1 blue) 20 blue	Rest	4 hours green Including 4 x (2 amber +10 blue poss on hills) To finish: 3 x flat-out sprints
8	Day off	60 mins green	Rest	60 mins green	Day off	Test	Rest

GETTING SERIOUS: FURTHER AND FASTER

If your cycling aims are to go faster and further, whether as a racer, a Sportive rider, or a tourist, you'll want to expand your riding week to take into account the kinds of durations and intensities your goals require. If you have limited time, you can adjust the seven-hour plan appropriately. For instance, go out on regular longer rides at the weekend if you're aiming for trips or events where you will be riding for five or six hours a day.

If you have time to increase your weekly training time further, then the next plan will take you up to 12 hours a week, allowing you to have a very solid endurance base and plenty of time for higher-quality work. Remember that longer, steady hours are still the important foundations of your fitness, but sessions around your functional threshold will boost your overall fitness levels, and the shorter intervals will improve things such as hill climbing and sprinting.

Use the blue/green sessions to practise your skills: cornering confidently, pedalling smoothly, changing gear effectively, or even your track stands! If you ride off-road, take time to study trails, how best to ride them, and practise, practise, practise. Learn to focus on your breathing and your pedalling, so that you're completely aware of all the processes and are cycling as efficiently as possible. Also concentrate on your thought processes and use the time to visualise your performance in your target events, especially if you intend to compete.

You may also wish to experiment and add variety to your sessions. For instance, replace intervals with one-legged riding (best done indoors, or quiet flat roads). Focus on using only your left leg for one minute, and then repeat with the right leg. This is not primarily aimed at improving the strength of your legs but improving your pedalling technique. Rather than pushing down on the pedals you should 'spin', trying to complete perfect circles. In theory, if you can pull up on the pedal on the opposite side to the downstroke this should markedly improve the force you can apply through the chain to the rear wheel. In practice this isn't very easy, and the best you can do is 'un-weight' the leg on the upstroke so that it detracts as little as possible from the push down on the opposite side.

Where you can improve significantly is to extend the force of the 'push' on the pedals further through the stroke. This will eliminate the 'dead spot' at the top and bottom of the stroke. For most people, improvements in efficiency can also be found by increasing the cadence above 90, or even to over 100 revs per minute. This is another technique you should try to incorporate into your training plans.

Remember, the purpose of training plans is to take you from A to B. So if your destination or goal is to ride faster time trials (see p. 146), make sure you're doing enough threshold riding. If you want to climb or sprint better, then incorporate those elements, or if your aim is to ride further or for longer, then focus on endurance hours.

For those of you who wish to race, a coach or an experienced friend can give you further advice on what areas you need to develop. You may wish to work on your weaknesses; so if you don't climb too well, work on that to improve your performance on hills. However, don't forget your strengths either: make the most of your natural abilities by working hard to maximise your advantage in those areas too.

WEEK	Mon	Tues	Weds	Thurs	Fri	Sat	Sun
1	Day off	60 mins 20 blue 10 yellow 5 blue 10 yellow 15 blue	60 mins blue	60 mins green	Rest	60 mins 10 blue 40 green 10 blue	3 hours green Including 1 x (15 yellow +10 blue)
2	Day off	90 mins 30 blue 15 yellow 10 blue 15 yellow 20 blue	60 mins blue	90 mins green	Rest	60 mins 10 blue 40 green 10 blue	3 hours green Including 2 x (15 yellow + 10 blue)
3	Day off	90 mins 30 blue 15 yellow 10 blue 15 yellow 20 blue	90 mins blue Use session to practise skills	90 mins green Including 5 x (60 secs red + 120 secs blue)	Rest	90 mins 15 blue 60 green 15 blue	3 hours green Including 3 x (15 yellow +10 blue)
4	Day off	2 hours 30 blue 15 yellow 10 blue 15 yellow 10 blue 30 green 10 blue	90 mins blue Use session to practise skills	2 hours green Including 5 x (60 secs red + 120 secs blue)	Rest	90 mins 15 blue 60 green 15 blue	3 hours green
5	Day off	2 hours 30 blue 15 yellow 10 blue 15 yellow 10 blue 30 green 10 blue	90 mins blue/green Use session to practise skills	2 hours green Including 5 x (60 secs red + 120 secs blue) 5 x (30 secs red + 30 secs blue)	Rest	2 hours 15 blue 90 green 15 blue	3 hours green Including 4 x (2 amber + 10 blue poss on hills)
6	Day off	2 hours 15 blue 30 green 15 blue 15 yellow 10 blue 15 yellow 20 blue	2 hours blue/green Use session to practise skills	2 hours green Including 5 x (30 secs red + 30 secs blue) 6 x (15 secs red + 45 secs blue)	Rest	2 hours 15 blue 90 green 15 blue	3 hours green Including 6 x (2 amber + 10 blue poss on hills)
7	Day off	2 hours 20 blue 30 green 15 yellow 10 blue 15 yellow 30 blue	2 hours blue/green Use session to practise skills	2 hours green Including 3 x (90 secs red + 90 blue) 6 x (15 secs red + 45 secs blue)	Rest	2 hours 15 blue 90 green 15 blue	4 hours green Including 1 x (15 yellow + 10 blue) 3 x (2 amber + 10 blue poss on hills)
8	Day off	60 mins green	Day off	90 mins green	Day off	Test	Rest

8:CROSS-TRAINING

The training plans in chapter 7 suggest that on some days you take part in other sports. So what might you do and how can that help your cycling?

Some professional riders adhere to the off-bike motto 'Don't stand if you can sit down, and don't sit if you can lie down!' It's a fair point if you're in the middle of a three-week tour racing four or more hours a day with barely enough time to recover in between. At other times, however, adding a different activity to your weekly schedule can be beneficial.

First, doing the same thing all the time can lead to a lack of mental freshness. No matter how much you love riding your bike, lots of cycling and nothing but cycling can lead to staleness and even reduce your motivation. Many riders feel it's best to have a short totally cycle-free period at some point of the year. Adding a different sport to your routine on a regular basis can also help to keep you fresh.

Certain elements of cycling impose very specific physical demands, and if you want to be a better cyclist, then cycling is the main way to improve. Even when you use the same muscles, you won't necessarily use them in quite the same way when performing non-cycling exercise. Running, for instance, uses some of the same main muscle groups in the lower half of the body. However, when you run muscles contract and lengthen, whereas when you cycle they shorten and lengthen. (Cyclists have a tendency to short hamstrings because we never fully extend our legs when pedalling.)

That doesn't mean that running is of no benefit at all. Like a number of other activities, it shares with cycling a huge reliance on cardio-vascular fitness. Any activity that increases the ability of your heart and lungs to perform more efficiently will have cross-sport benefits. This is especially true if your fitness is at a very low level. When you first begin an exercise regime you will find you gain greater benefits and improvements by cross-training, while the fitter and more targeted you become on cycling performance, then the more important cycle-specific training becomes.

There are two particular areas where I train off the bike and where there are real benefits to improving my performance on the bike: strength training and flexibility training.

TIP

If you're not used to gym work, always start with low weights and get advice from a gym instructor or an experienced friend to make sure you do the exercises in the correct way; otherwise you risk injury.

STRENGTH TRAINING

Some cyclists avoid gym sessions altogether, others use them mainly during the winter months, and some see the value of weight training throughout much of the year. I certainly benefit from incorporating strength training into my training regime, and that doesn't always mean having to go the gym.

You can break down the benefits of strength training into two categories: direct specific improvements to cycling muscle groups, and complementary benefits to riding performance. There is some debate about how much increasing the amount of weight you can raise with a squat lift improves anything other than your ability to perform squats with bigger weights. While the action in itself is different from pedalling, you should find some improvements with the right approach. The advantages include an increase in muscle mass, and also in the ability of the muscle to resist fatigue. Increasing non-functional muscle mass could, of course, be counter-productive for cyclists, especially climbers, where unnecessary weight is a major limiting factor. But this will be far less important for track sprinters, who can gain more benefits from explosive muscle strength, and for whom total power output has more significance than the power-to-weight ratio that is the key to successful riding on hilly terrain.

Resistance training that is designed to delay the onset of muscle fatigue can have significant benefits for cycling, but remember to maintain a balance across your training load. Spend too much time in the gym, especially when you're putting in a lot of bike time, and you can easily become at best stale, and even worse, risk being over-trained. If you find your legs feel tired and 'heavy', then ease up on the weights.

TIP

If you're highly trained or very fit in one activity, it's easy to imagine that you will be able to push yourself at a similar level in another area. This can lead you to under-estimate the effort involved and consequently risk injury. You should therefore take care when switching sports, especially if you're close to an important objective in your cycling plan.

LOWER BODY STRENGTHENING

The best machines to use in the gym for lower body strengthening are the leg press, hamstring curl and leg extension. There are also machines to help you with squats, which can also be done with free weights. The squat uses the entire upper leg muscle groups and is therefore the most effective of these.

You can practise the motion itself at home, and to begin with you may find that in itself is a good work-out. Once in the gym, add an empty bar and then gradually increase weights as you improve the strength in your legs. Like all free weights, it's of paramount importance that you do this exercise correctly with good 'form', rather than struggle to lift a bar that is too heavy. Hold the bar across your shoulders with your feet slightly wider than your hips and pointing straight forward, or possibly angled out just a little. Keep your back straight, bend your legs and lower your hips until your thighs are parallel to the floor, then push up to return to the standing position.

TIP

When you do squats you should have a partner to 'spot' you. This person is there to help steady you or take the weight if you struggle to make the lift.

As a general rule, aim to do between eight and twelve repetitions, or lifts, in each 'set' of exercises. After a short rest, repeat the same number of squats, and then repeat them again, to make three sets. If you find you can easily manage twelve repetitions, then increase the weight by around 10 per cent. Once you become more experienced you can do three sets where you increase the weight and decrease the number of repetitions by two each time. Alternatively, try a 'pyramid' set of five, where you ramp up the weight on sets two and three, and then reduce each time for sets four and five.

UPPER BODY STRENGTHENING AND CORE STABILITY

As cyclists, it's easy to focus on the legs and forget the upper body. However, anyone new to cycling will quickly find out that a long ride can put a great deal of strain on arms, shoulders and neck. Clearly, once you become fatigued in these areas you're going to find it harder to handle the bike, and the strain is also going to affect the efficiency of the lower half of your body, as well as having a psychological impact on the remainder of your ride.

It's therefore worth considering a regular routine to improve the strength of your neck, shoulder, back, chest and arm muscles. Press-ups and tricep dips can be done almost anywhere, along with shoulder shrugs. With a few small weights (even tins of baked beans!) you can add bicep curls without going to the gym. If you do have access to a fitness centre with a rowing machine, then a seated row is good all-round exercise for most of these muscle groups.

Even more important is core strength. In recent years, athletes in most sports have come to discover the benefits of the solid foundation provided by trunk muscles. With a strong core, the limbs can work better. When the core is stable there is less movement, so less energy is wasted. And when our bodies are kept in balance by the deep muscles at their centre, there is less likelihood of injury. But the problem with core muscles is that they lie deep within the body and are difficult to access. Other forms of fitness training will have little or no effect on these muscles, and therefore they have to be specifically targeted if you want to reap the major benefits that a strong stable core can give.

Don't confuse core stability conditioning with traditional sit-ups, which target some abdominal muscles in the quest for a 'six pack'. Instead, the focus is on the muscles that are attached to the spine and around the pelvis. Improve your core stability and you will find you can produce more power when you ride. More than that, you will also have better posture both on and off the bike, improving comfort and helping to prevent injury; in particular, it will help if you suffer from stiffness or discomfort in the back.

Even better news is that it needn't be a time-consuming addition to your daily routine, and while the large inflatable 'Swiss balls' that you find in gyms can be used, you can still do many of the exercises with no special equipment. What is important is to learn the correct techniques. The muscles you're training, such as the transversus abdominis and the multifidus, are not ones that you can see, and most of us cannot naturally identify them by feel. Finding the right postures to develop endurance in these muscles is an important precursor to undertaking more dynamic core exercises, and unless you have the correct foundation you won't get the full advantage of core stability training.

You can get hands-on advice on how to perform these positions and actions at many gyms, especially if they run yoga or Pilates classes. Pilates is in fact one of the best off-bike activities to incorporate into your training programme, with its emphasis not only on core stability, but also on flexibility and relaxation. If you can find a local Pilates class, or at least a Pilates video, I would highly recommend it.

The first element of these exercises is to find your neutral spine position. Lie on your back, feet flat on the floor, with your knees bent. Make sure your hips, legs and feet are parallel, with your arms resting at your side. Your spine should be neither arched, nor flat against the floor, but there should be just a small gap into which you can fit your fingers.

Plank

Relax, and breathe deeply, then try this exercise. Breathe out and pull in your lower abdomen, forcing your belly button towards the floor. If you're not sure whether you're doing it correctly, imagine the action required to zip up a pair of jeans that are too tight! Hold this contraction for ten seconds, but stay relaxed and make sure you continue to breathe normally. You don't have to pull too hard – it's stamina you're after, not strength – and make sure you're only contracting your lower abdomen, not the upper abdominals (your 'six pack').

Once you're confident with this manoeuvre, try it out in different positions: lying on your front, sitting and standing. Remember this position and maintain it while performing dynamic core stability exercises and also introduce it to your cycling.

Two of the most effective core strength exercises that you can perform just about anywhere are the plank and the side plank.

Lie face down, with your elbows and forearms under your chest and pointing straight forward. Lift your body off the ground so that it's supported on your forearms (with your elbows bent at 90 degrees) and on the balls of your feet. Make sure your body is stretched out, your legs together and your back flat. Ensuring that your hips don't sag, breathe normally and focus on tightening your core abdominal muscles. Hold this for as long as you can maintain a flat 'bridge'.

FACT

If you cycle regularly, you can expect to be as fit as an average person ten years younger.

Side plank

This is the same exercise but now rotated either clockwise or counter-clockwise through 90 degrees. One side or the other is now facing downwards, with your weight supported by one arm (which is still bent at the elbow and pointing forwards from your chest) and the side of one foot. Your upper foot should be placed on top of the lower, with your non-supporting arm along your upper side. Make sure your hips don't sag forwards or downwards, and keep your body in line.

FLEXIBILITY TRAINING

One of the major advantages of yoga or Pilates routines is that they can provide you not only with added core strength but also increased flexibility. Being more flexible has several benefits. It gives you more scope to adopt different riding positions. This can improve comfort, pedalling efficiency and, especially for time triallists, give major gains in terms of greater aerodynamics. Flexible muscle groups can also have more strength and are less prone to injury. As we've seen already, the way that we cycle can in itself reduce flexibility; the fact that our legs never fully extend in the pedalling motion is a contributory factor to shorter hamstrings with a less than optimum range of extension.

Stretching should in fact be a part of your everyday life, and certainly a key component of every ride. Stretching before a ride can help you to ride better and also play a part in avoiding injury, as will post-ride stretching. Time spent on this after riding will not only develop flexibility but will also combat fatigue and aid recovery. There are two priorities after riding:

first, to remove the build-up of exercise-induced toxicity in muscles, and secondly, to introduce nutrients to restore and rebuild. Both are heightened by greater blood flow, which is improved by post-ride stretching. You will therefore feel less sore and fresher next time if you don't see the end of the ride as the end of your session.

TIP

For both pre- and post-ride stretches you only need five or ten minutes. Get used to doing it regularly, make it a habit, and you'll soon do it automatically and reap the benefits that it brings.

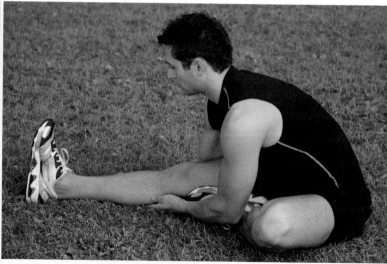

Hamstrings

Quads

These are the muscles on the front of the thigh that do a huge part of the cycling effort. Using your right hand to stabilise yourself, stand on your right leg and grasp your left ankle with your left hand. Standing straight pull your left foot gently up towards your bottom so that your knee bends and you feel the stretch down the front of your thigh. Hold for 20–30 seconds and then repeat on the right leg.

The hamstring is the muscle at the back of the upper leg, and one that cyclists can most benefit from stretching. One way of doing this is to stand and lift one leg onto a wall, chair or similar surface a little lower than the height of your hips. Make sure it's the correct height so that you can stand in neutral alignment. Keep your standing foot and your hips and shoulders pointing forwards, and with your hands on the thigh of the extended leg lean forward through your hips. Repeat for the opposite side. Alternatively, sit on the floor with one leg extended and the other bent at 90 degrees. Lean forward through the hips, as above, to feel the stretch in the hamstring of the extended leg, ensuring you keep your back straight.

Calves

Standing upright, lean against something sturdy, like a wall, with your arms outstretched. With both your knees slightly bent, put your left foot slightly forward, and your right foot slightly back. Keeping both feet flat on the floor, push your right leg forward over your foot so that you feel the stretch in your right calf. Repeat for the opposite leg.

Back

You can stretch your back quite simply by bending 90 degrees at the waist, leaning forward to reach out with one hand on your saddle and the other on your bike's handlebars. Keep your feet a shoulder-width apart and your torso parallel to the ground (see photo top left). Alternatively, lie on your back and curl both knees up to your chest, gently pulling in on the front of your knees to extend the stretch (see top right). An additional back stretch is to lie flat with both arms on the ground. Then bring each leg in turn over to the ground at a 90-degree angle from your body, using your hand to hold it there if necessary. Keep your shoulders on the ground (see left).

Your buttock muscles play a big part in cycling; the gluteus maximus is the largest muscle in the human body. Lie on your back with your knees bent and feet flat on the floor. Place your right ankle at the end of your left thigh on top of the knee. With your hand behind your left knee, pull your legs towards your shoulders so that your feel the stretch on the outside of your right buttock, and repeat on the opposite side.

Glutes

Hip flexors

This stretch is similar to a lunge. Put your left leg forward and your right leg back. Keep your torso upright and your right foot flat on the floor while pushing your left hip. This stretches the right hip flexor, and you can extend the stretch further by bending your left knee (see left). Hold and carefully return to a standing position and then repeat for the opposite side.

There are often a number of alternatives for stretches, and some may suit you better than others. You will also find a range of stretches for a number of other muscles, so investigate via books or the internet. But if in doubt take advice from experts and make sure you do any exercises safely and correctly. Just as with strength training, cheating and cutting corners to try and achieve a longer stretch will not only mean you're not actually gaining the desired benefit, but you could also injure yourself.

It is important to remember that stretching shouldn't hurt! It's not a competition to see how much pain you can inflict on yourself by pushing your muscle to an extreme. The idea is to gently stretch the muscle as far as it will comfortably go. You will find that the more you do, the further you'll be able to stretch, but don't be tempted to damage your muscles by extending them beyond their capable range. The movements should also be slow and smooth. Don't bounce! Jerky movements could do the opposite of what you're trying to achieve and increase the risk of muscle damage. You should aim to hold stretches for 20–30 seconds.

WARMING UP

You can compare your muscles with rubber bands. Try this experiment. Put a rubber band in the freezer for a while and see how far it stretches. You will find that not only does it not extend as much when it's cold, it is also more brittle and more likely to snap. Warm the band up and you'll find that its ability to stretch is enhanced. The important lesson is to warm up before you begin your stretches. Five minutes of gentle aerobic exercise on the bike, or perhaps jogging or skipping, will raise your core body temperature by a couple of degrees and increase blood flow to the muscles.

RUNNING

Like cycling, running relies heavily on cardio-respiratory performance, and is therefore a good alternative if you can't (or don't wish to) ride your bike for a period. It gives a number of cross-benefits. However, unlike cycling, where you rest on the saddle and handlebars, running is not weight supported. The up-side of this is that it places a heavier load on your body. It therefore stresses your heart and lungs more and burns more calories. If you're time limited, then you may find that for short sessions you can get more benefit from a short run than a short cycle ride.

There are other benefits too. It may be the ideal alternative if you're away from home without access to your bike. It also has advantages in bad weather: you can come straight back from a run, throw your kit in the wash and jump straight in the shower, without worrying about cleaning down a bike. It also saves time – there's no need to get together all your cycling kit and pump up the tyres before you set off. If you only have an hour to spare in a busy life, you may be lucky to get around half an hour on the bike, by the time you're actually ready to start riding. However, you could run a hard 45-minute session, which would be the equivalent of more than an hour and a half's riding.

Weight-bearing exercise like running is also an important part of maintaining bone density. Even extensively trained cyclists may suffer from bone thinning because they spend so much time on the bike and little or no time doing the kind of exercise that can protect against osteoporosis. Low bone densities increase the risk of fractures, so running (and also weight training) can help combat this problem.

On the other hand, there are potential pitfalls. During the early part of your cycling training, running may improve your cycling by improving heart and lung performance. Developing muscles not specifically trained by cycling but complementary to it may also see you riding better. However, the longer you've been cycling and the higher the level of your cycling performance, then the fewer benefits you're likely to receive from running, other than it being a good way to maintain some fitness while taking a well-earned mental break from a long cycling season.

If you've ever tried running you may have been pleasantly surprised the following day to find that you didn't have any aches and pains, only to feel really stiff and sore a day later. This is quite common for first-time runners and will ease once you start running regularly, but don't be tempted to run too far and too fast too soon. Being able to ride a bike doesn't mean you can automatically transfer the same level of performance to a different exercise, so don't be disheartened if it doesn't match that of your friends in the local running club. It's also worth pointing out that the occasional run here and there isn't going to improve your ability on two legs, so if you wish to become a better runner, you'll need to do it regularly.

RUNNING SHOES
Running may not require the range of equipment and associated costs involved in cycling, but there is one key piece of kit that is vital, and one on which you shouldn't skimp. Ill-fitting and non-supportive running shoes can cause injury problems, and ideally you should visit a specialist shop, where your gait can be analysed and appropriate footwear recommended.

SWIMMING

Heading to the pool can be a good complement to cycling. Like riding a bike, it's weight supported, reducing the potential for injury. It also provides a good work-out for your upper body, which can improve your ability to hold yourself stable and comfortable when back on the bike. It's also worth noting that your resting heart rate will drop by around 10 beats a minute once in the water, and your maximum heart rate by twice that amount. You should take this into account if you intend to use your heart rate as a basis for training while swimming.

TRIATHLON

If you enjoy running and swimming, as well as cycling, why not have a go at Triathlon! A combination of all three, Triathlons normally start with a swim, followed by a bike ride and finish with a run. The short-distance Sprint Triathlon is 750m in the water, 20km riding and a 5km run. As a 'fun' competition outside the racing season, or an alternative challenge for Sportive riders, this could be a different way to add some fresh motivation. However, if you get the bug and are tempted by an 'Ironman' you'll have to swim 3.8km, ride 180km and then run a full 26-mile (42.2km) marathon. If you commit to that kind of schedule you're no longer a cyclist doing some cross-training but a full-on Triathlete!

SPINNING

Not exactly cross-training, since you are of course on a bike, but spinning on stationary cycles has developed from the exercise classes offered in gyms. Riding in a small or large group, you follow the lead of an instructor in a session normally lasting between 45 minutes and an hour. This is usually accompanied by music which, along with the instructions of the group leader, and the communal feel of the session, can help with motivation.

Spin classes will provide you with a good cardio-vascular training session, and will provide a more cycling-specific work-out than other gym machines or running. Because you can adjust the resistance on the bikes, everyone can take the session at their own level, even in a mixed-ability class. Put the effort in and you will certainly get a good work-out.

TIP

The instructor should take you through stretching warm-up and cool-down; if not, make sure that you give yourself time to prepare properly for the class.

In the winter months when it's dark and wet, or when you're time restricted, spinning or studio cycling can be a good alternative to getting out on your bike. It's also a useful way of building up initial fitness for novice cyclists, and provides an indoor option if you don't have your own indoor turbo-trainer. Some people find group classes a far more appealing prospect than a solo session on the turbo.

On the other hand, there are drawbacks. Although some adjustments are possible on spin bikes, they will never have quite the same set-up as your road bike. If you're following a carefully worked out training plan, the session probably won't provide the exact specific elements of your programme. Classes tend to be fairly intensive, so make sure you're still getting plenty of lower-level endurance riding too.

Although spinning will help train your heart, lungs and legs, indoor riding does nothing to improve your bike handling skills – another good reason to get out on your bike if you can.

As with the turbo-trainer, spin classes make you sweat! With no movement and cold air to cool you, you'll need a good towel and plenty of water to drink when you join spinning sessions. Wear a thin vest or T-shirt and a pair of cycling shorts, but you will probably also have to wear trainers as most studio bikes have pedals with toe clips.

CROSS-COUNTRY SKIING/SKATING

Both cross-country skiing and skating share similar muscle groups and movements with cycling. They may use some of the muscles in a slightly different way, but that can be beneficial in developing complementary functional fitness. Like running, they will both provide a substantial cardio-vascular work-out to help improve or maintain your endurance on the bike. The advantage over running is their low-impact nature on knees and ankles.

Of course, to go cross-country skiing you need snow, but you can get similar benefits from elliptical trainers in the gym. However, I love cross-country skiing – it's one of my favourite off-bike activities!

REMEMBER:

- If you want to improve your bike riding, cycling is the best way to do it.
- Stretching, warming up and cooling down should be seen as part of the training routine.
- If you do add other sports to your routine, then take that into account in your overall exercise totals. Don't overload yourself.
- Always approach new disciplines with care, and if necessary seek some expert advice.

9:NUTRITION AND HEALTH

Your body is the engine to power your cycling and the fuel you put in it is therefore very important. What you eat and drink can have a major impact on your cycling performance, and while the normal basic rules of healthy eating apply, there are certain extra considerations to take into account if you're a regular cyclist, along with particular requirements when you're actually on the bike.

Nutrition (and hydration, because drinking adequately is equally important) is a huge and often complicated subject. We are consequently being given new (and sometimes conflicting) advice about general dietary requirements, and there is a constant barrage of studies updating accepted sports science wisdom. It's not difficult to find different research findings that seem to prove opposing claims.

Some riders pack their diet with all the latest recommended supplements, carefully measure and weigh their food intake, and devour every possible new finding that could give them a little extra advantage. If you can (and wish) to follow that course, there are plenty of resources to keep you at the cutting edge. The purpose of this chapter is simply to give you a general introduction and some basic guidelines to help you get the most out of your cycling.

TIP
The good news is that cycling uses plenty of calories, so you can eat more, but it can also give you a huge appetite, so make sure you don't overdo it at a café stop when out riding with friends or club mates!

ENERGY USE

So how much fuel do we need? Each and every second of every day our bodies are burning calories just to live. You need energy to breathe, to think, and to keep all your other body systems functioning; the amount of energy needed for this is your 'basal metabolic rate' (BMR). This varies by sex, age and weight, and will also be higher for those with a higher percentage of muscle compared to body fat. We can, however, work out an approximate BMR, which gives a starting point in calculating our daily calorific requirements.

Age	Women	Men
10–17:	(weight x 12.2) + 746	(weight x 17.5) + 651
18–30:	(weight x 14.7) + 496	(weight x 15.3) + 679
31–60:	(weight x 8.7) + 829	(weight x 11.6) + 879
Over 60	(weight x 10.5) + 596	(weight x 13.5) + 487

1. Weigh yourself in kilograms (or convert your weight from pounds by dividing it by 2.25).
2. Use the range of formulae in the box above to calculate your BMR. For example, for me aged 25 with a weight of 58kg, the calculation is as follows:

(58 x 14.7) + 496 = 1349

In other words, if I do nothing but sleep and slump in front of the TV all day I'll use 1349 calories. Of course I do a lot more than that! In order to find the number of calories I burn doing normal daily activities, I can use the following Physical Activity Quotients (PAQ):

Very light activity (sitting in cafés with friends, driving, using the computer, etc.): BMR x 1.5

Light activity (easy housework, walking slowly, shopping): BMR x 2.5

Moderate activity (dancing, brisk walking, playing tennis): BMR x 5.0

Heavy activity (climbing stairs, active sports, walking quickly): BMR x 7.0

Imagine a routine (non-training day) was made up as follows:
12 hours resting (12 x 1 = 12)
8 hours very light activity (8 x 1.5 = 12)
2 hours light activity (2 x 2.5 = 5)
1 hour moderate activity (1 x 5 = 5)
1 hour heavy activity (1 x 7 = 7)

My PAQ would therefore be 41 ÷ 24 hours = 1.71

Now I just multiply my BMR by my PAQ (1349 x 1.71) to discover that on a non-training day I would use 2307 calories.

To find out how many calories I use on a training day I can work out the calories I use according to my PAQ for 20 hours, using the activity guide above (perhaps 21 ÷ 20 = 1.05), which would mean 1349 x 1.05 = 1416 calories, and then add my calories for the training period (say 3400), to give a total calorie expenditure on that day of 4816 calories (normally expressed as kcal – kilocalories).

One of the advantages of training with a power meter, heart rate monitor or bike computer is that it will provide you with a figure for the number of calories used. If you don't have access to that information, you can approximate energy used as follows.

Speed (on flat)	Calories burned per hour
10mph	133
15mph	349
20mph	742
25mph	1374
30mph	2303

That's enough maths for now! What do we do with the figures? We now know that on a particular training day I used around 4800 calories. I therefore need to put back into the system the same number in order to maintain my current bodyweight.

Providing the right balance of calories ingested to calories burnt is important. Unused calories have to be stored, and if you regularly take in more than you use, you'll see your weight and fat levels grow. If you consistently have a negative energy balance, then your weight will fall. That might be an attractive prospect if you feel you could slim down a little. If you regularly tackle hilly terrain you'll certainly appreciate not carrying unnecessary pounds, and if you're racing you may wish to reduce your body fat percentage to quite a low level in order to maximise your power-to-weight ratio.

However, you should exercise caution when it comes to weight loss. In the example above, suppose I only put back in 3800 calories, a negative energy balance of 1000. A substantial shortfall like that is unlikely to provide the refuelling necessary for my body to make the optimal adaptations to the training stress it's just received. It's also unlikely to recover fully and re-establish sufficient energy levels for me to train properly the next day. If you consistently under-fuel to that extent you will soon feel tired and will probably be less motivated too. You're also likely to compromise your immune system, thus running the risk of illness. And then if you don't train your fitness will drop and quite possibly your weight will actually rise!

If you do feel you need to lose weight, you should aim for a negative energy balance that doesn't exceed 15 per cent. In my example above that would have been a deficit of 720 calories. This is more than adequate for sensible weight reduction. A daily shortfall of 500 calories will equal 3500 in a week, and

LOSING WEIGHT
- Keep a separate food diary for a week or add the information to your training diary. You can then see exactly how many calories and other nutrients you take on board and what changes you may need to make.
- If you're planning on losing weight, work out 15 per cent of your daily calorific expenditure, equate that to specific elements of your diet, and devise a strategy for cutting down.
- Look at the foods you currently eat and consider if there are any changes you could make that would support your riding needs better.

You may have heard people talking about 'fat-burning' zones. The idea is that since bodies burn fat during lower-intensity exercise, but not once the exercise gets really hard, then to specifically shift fat you should do long, slow, steady sessions. Recent research, however, has contradicted this, suggesting that short, high-intensity rides, such as intervals, will burn more calories and therefore reduce weight quicker.

that should equate to losing one pound or around half a kilogram. If you do have a target event (a touring holiday, Sportive or important hilly race) by which you hope to have reached a certain point on the scales, give yourself enough time to reach it sensibly. That way you won't compromise your health and fitness.

FUELING YOUR BODY – WHAT SHOULD YOU EAT?

We've looked at how much fuel you need; the next thing to consider is the type of fuel. What we eat can be split into three main groups: fats, carbohydrates and protein. These are stored and then converted to adenosine triphosphate (ATP).

In order to make muscles contract, the body releases energy from the breakdown of ATP by using one of three energy pathways.

- For low-intensity, long-duration exercise it uses oxygen to convert fat, carbohydrate and sometimes protein into ATP. This is aerobic exercise and can continue for hours, but energy production is quite slow.

- At higher intensities the body can produce ATP more rapidly by breaking down glycogen without the use of oxygen. This leads to the production of lactic acid (at the point known as the lactate threshold), which can also be recycled as ATP. Muscle pain and fatigue limit this anaerobic exercise to a couple of minutes.
- The third pathway is to use ATP directly, but only enough for two or three seconds' exercise can be stored, after which more is synthesised from creatine phosphate (CP), which runs out after six to eight seconds. A very-high-intensity short burst of around ten seconds is therefore possible with ATP–CP exercise before the body has to switch to one of the other two metabolic mechanisms.

Part of the process of training your body is to encourage it to use fat more often, more efficiently and to a higher level of intensity, thus sparing your glycogen reserves for when they are really necessary. The fat we eat is stored around our bodies, either in our muscles or as adipose tissue. Carbohydrates are stored either as glucose in the blood or glycogen in muscles, with any excess being turned to fat. Unwanted protein is also converted to fat after it has been used for its primary purpose of building muscle. Protein is only used as fuel once glycogen stores have been depleted.

CARBOHYDRATES
Carbohydrates fall into two categories. Simple sugars (found, for example, in fruit juices and energy drinks) are quickly converted to blood glucose, providing rapidly available energy. Complex carbohydrates are starches (such as whole-grain cereals used in pasta and bread), and these take longer to digest before being converted into glycogen. A full glycogen store is normally enough for around 1–1.5 hours' exercise, after which you can suffer what cyclists call 'the bonk' if you don't top it up.

It's important therefore that you get adequate carbohydrate levels before, during and after your ride. In fact research has not only shown that physical performance is better with adequate carbohydrate intake, but that it also enhances feelings of pleasure both during and after prolonged periods of cycling. This is perhaps not so surprising, since the brain runs on

INDEX	SUGAR	DAIRY	FRUIT	GRAIN	VEGETABLES
High GI foods					
100+	Alcohol		Dates		Parsnip
90-100	Glucose Sport Drinks				
80-89	Jelly Beans			White Rice Cornflakes	Baked Potato Mashed Potato
70-79	Jam		Watermelon	Wheat, Cereals Whole Wheat Bread	French Fries
Medium GI foods					
60-69	Soft Drink Sucrose Honey	Ice Cream	Pineapple Raisins Bananas	Couscous Brown Rice Muesli Pasta	
50-59	Chocolate		Mango Kiwi	Sweetcorn Pastry Porrridge Oats Rye Bread	Sweet Potato Popcorn Crisps Cooked Carrots
Low GI foods					
40-49			Orange Juice Apple Juice Grapes	Oatmeal Spaghetti Whole Wheat Pasta	Baked Beans
30-49		Butter Milk Yogurt	Apples Pears Strawberries Unripe Banana	Rye	Tomato Soup Chick Peas Split Peas
Under 30	Fructose		Peaches Grapefruit Cherries	Barley	Kidney Beans Lentils Uncooked Carrots Greens Peanuts

glucose. Without enough glucose you can feel dizzy, and both mental and physical function will deteriorate.

How much carbohydrate do you need? In general, you should have 4–5g per kilogram of bodyweight every day if you cycle is at a moderate level, 6–7g if you have a heavier training load, and up to 8–9g per kilogram for elite riders. A cyclist in regular training for a Sportive and weighing 65kg would require 390–455g of carbohydrate a day. As an example, a medium banana would provide around 27g, a jacket potato 36g, a plate of pasta 40g, and a bowl of porridge 65g.

To help you decide which carbohydrates are best you can refer to the glycaemic index. This ranks food from 0 to 100 based on how quickly it causes blood sugar levels to rise compared with pure glucose (which is ranked 100). Anything with a GI of 50 or under is considered low, 51–69 is medium GI, and 70 or above is rated high. A combination of low- and high-GI foods is fine an hour or two before exercise; high to provide instant energy from the start of your ride, and slower-release lower-GI carbohydrates to sustain your energy levels during the ride. After your ride you need rapid recovery, so go for high GI foods such as white bread, baked potatoes or a 'recovery drink'.

Recovery

It's long been held that after exercise there is a 'window' of opportunity, up to a couple of hours, during which depleted glycogen stores are extra receptive to replenishment. While some evidence suggests that such a short timescale is less crucial than many believe, nonetheless it makes sense in the immediate post-exercise period to refuel your body, along with re-hydrating it.

Adequate recovery means not only replacing lost fluids and replenishing glycogen levels, but also supplying protein for muscle development. There are a number of natural foods you can turn to for this: orange juice and a white bread sandwich or a baked potato with a high-protein filling would be fine for this purpose. You can also buy specific sports 'recovery drinks'. Although these can be expensive, they guarantee not only to give you the right levels of carbohydrate and protein, but also to replenish lost vitamins, minerals and fluids. Drinking for recovery is ideal for those who find their appetite is suppressed after exercise, and if the drink is available as soon as you get back from riding you can drink it while cooling down and stretching.

TIP

If you're a competitive cyclist and you choose to take supplements, including sports drinks, be fully aware of all the ingredients to make sure none are on the list of banned substances. Some governing bodies will keep a list of products known to be acceptable, so get advice, and if in doubt don't take a risk. Choose a known safe alternative or manage without.

In-ride re-fuelling

Glycogen stores will run out 60–90 minutes into your ride, and fat can only be used on its own as a fuel for very-low-intensity activity. Anybody who has found themselves a long way from home when the body's fuel tank hits zero will know what an unpleasant feeling it can be. So how do you avoid 'the bonk' or 'hunger knock'? Because the body can synthesise carbohydrate (especially simple sugars) quite quickly, you should keep topping up throughout the ride. If your session is less than an hour long, then you shouldn't need to worry about anything other than hydration, so plain water is fine. If you intend to ride for longer, start taking more carbohydrates on board after about half an hour and continue to regularly drip feed throughout the ride.

You have two choices, solids or liquids. A pocketful of dried fruit is an ideal way to regularly top up with easily accessible energy, or you may wish to use specially formulated sports energy bars. These come in a whole variety of types; some will suit you better than others, so experiment and see which you prefer. Some people find it difficult to eat solid foods while riding, in which case carbohydrate drinks can provide all your refuelling requirements. These have the additional advantage of providing hydration, and some also replace the salts you lose through sweat. Because you can sip them regularly they tend to be a more convenient solution than eating, although on long rides you may feel the physical need to have something a little more substantial in your stomach, so most riders use a combination of both food and drinks.

There is also one other half-and-half option – energy gels. These commercially available sachets are packed full of instant-hit sugars – ideal for emergency fuelling or providing the boost for blasting through the last half-hour of a ride. If you use them, make sure you take on board plenty of fluid at the same time.

The exact amount of carbohydrate you need to consume on the bike depends of course on your own metabolism and the intensity of the exercise you're doing. You will need 30–60g of carbohydrate per hour, and in drink a solution of around 4–8 per cent. Use slightly lower concentrations in hot weather, when your fluid replenishment needs will be higher.

HYDRATION

It's sometimes easy to forget to drink on the bike, whether because you're chatting with friends or have your head down going flat out in a race. It is, however, vital before, during and after riding; our bodies are, after all, almost two-thirds water. A relatively small fall in hydration levels can have significant effects on performance. Some studies show a 25 per cent drop in performance with a 4 per cent drop in hydration.

If you've ever weighed yourself before and after a long ride you may have noticed a drop of perhaps a kilogram or more in weight. This will largely be fluid loss! It's important that you don't just rely on feeling thirsty to prompt you to drink (this mechanism can be suppressed during exercise); you must get into the automatic habit of sipping regularly.

DELIVERING LIQUID

Most road riders tend to use bottles in cages attached to their frames, but you can also get liquid pouches holding up to several litres, which you wear in a backpack. These are especially popular with mountain bikers because you drink by sucking from a valve which can be placed near the mouth. There's no need to take your hands off the handlebars with these systems.

If you use a bottle in a cage, make sure you practise taking it in and out so you can drink without it having too much effect on your riding. If you're riding in a large group, dropping a water bottle can have undesired consequences! Be sensible, too, about where you drink. Climbing might make you very thirsty, but there's no point in reaching for the bottle and disrupting your rhythm just before the summit. Waiting until you're over the top is a better choice for a well-earned drink.

The general recommendation for all adults is to drink two litres of fluid a day, and if you eat more than average (as cyclists tend to do), your fluid requirements will also increase, even before you consider replacing the fluid lost while actually riding. You should then drink at least half a litre (one small cycling water bottle) for every hour of riding. This figure can double in hot weather and with higher-intensity exercise.

If you're in an organised Sportive event there will be regular re-fuelling stops where you can re-fill your bottles (along with food for your pockets). In races, you should have somebody to hand you up fresh bottles in the designated feed zones, and if you're out on long training rides, make sure there are places where you can stop to replenish your bottles.

Getting the balance right is of course important. Drinking too much can cause unscheduled stops (and even in extreme cases severe mental dysfunction due to low sodium concentrations). You can tell if you're not drinking enough if, on a visit to the toilet, there's mild burning or your urine is darker than a very pale yellow.

Don't stop drinking once you've finished your ride. Continue for the next few hours, gradually taking in at least half a litre for each hour of your exercise session. Of course, as already discussed, this can be combined with glycogen replacement and also taking on board proteins to aid recovery. Proteins are made up of amino acids, and if you do use a commercial recovery formula, choosing one which includes branched-chain amino acids (BCAAs) could enhance muscle repair.

PROTEIN

Protein is another area of nutrition where research seems to ebb and flow.

Different studies and different schools of thought vary on whether athletes and active people need more protein or not.

Current daily intake recommendations for endurance athletes vary from 1.4 to 1.8g of protein for every kilogram of bodyweight, dependent on how much riding you're actually doing on any given day. If you weigh 65kg, this translates into 91–117g of protein a day. The table shows the amount of protein given by typical servings of some common foods.

As with many areas of nutrition, more is not necessarily better. There is evidence that getting too much of your food in the form of protein (as in some weight-loss plans or body-building regimes) can be dangerous. Eating more protein than your body needs for building muscle will mean that the excess is burned for energy or converted immediately to fat. Excessively high intakes, however (more than 20 per cent of the total energy in the diet), are linked to various medical problems, including kidney stones and increased loss of calcium from the body.

Food (typical serving)	Protein (grams)
Steak	26
Chicken	22
Kidney beans	16
Lentils	16
Skimmed milk (half pint)	10
Cheddar cheese	7
Egg	6
Almonds	6
Tofu	6
Wholemeal bread (2 slices)	5

In terms of energy delivery, your daily intake of calories should be broken down roughly as follows: 65 per cent carbohydrate, 20 per cent fat and 15 per cent protein.

FATS

For many people 'fat' is a 'dirty' word – it's the excess bits in various places that we want to get rid of. It shouldn't be. For a start, fat on the body plays an important role in a number of ways, including storing Vitamin E. You may hear about elite athletes with body fat percentages as low as 4 or 5 per cent. That doesn't mean it's necessarily suitable for you, and there are equally successful female endurance athletes with percentages in the normal healthy adult range, which rises to 30 per cent in women.

Just as we all have different heights, shapes, heart rates and other vital statistics, so we all have our own optimum range of fat levels. Trying to achieve an artificially low level will be counter-productive, especially in women, where it can cause amenorrhoea (irregular or stopped periods) and premature osteoporosis.

As already outlined, fat is part of the fuel mix for endurance athletes, and the right training can ensure it has an increased role in energy production. Although carbohydrate and protein can be turned into fat, we do also need dietary sources. Not all fat are the same, however, and they have a bigger role than just providing calories.

- **Trans-fats:** It's generally accepted that there are good fats and bad fats, and trans-fats definitely fall into the latter category. They are created artificially through hydrogenation and appear in highly processed foods and some margarines. While they have many benefits for food manufacturers, they have no nutritional value whatsoever. They also reduce good cholesterol, raise bad cholesterol and have been linked with many negative effects, including cell damage. Where possible, avoid trans-fats completely.
- **Saturated fats:** These are often seen as bad, but they do have some dietary value. They are found mainly in animal sources like meat, eggs and dairy products. Consuming too much of saturated fats has been linked to raised cholesterol levels, weight gain and increased risk of heart disease; it's best to limit their consumption to no more than 10 per cent of your daily calorific intake. It is, however, worth noting that these animal foods also contain a type of fat known as conjugated linoleic acid (CLA), which has been shown to encourage muscle growth, reduce body fat and

protect from muscle loss during dieting. CLA is also available as a supplement.
- **Unsaturated fats:** The third type of fats are the good guys. Unsaturated fats come in two types, polyunsaturated (Omega 3 and 6) and mono-unsaturated (Omega 9).

  The polyunsaturated fats promote weight loss, and keep us both physically and mentally healthy. Omega 3 is the fat in oily fish which is why your grandmother probably told you to eat fish if you wanted to be brainy! Flax oil is another good source, and dark green vegetables also have small amounts of Omega 3. Omega 6 fats are found in many nuts and oils, and a healthy recommendation is to have three times more Omega 6 fats compared with Omega 3. In Western diets, processed foods and fast foods use large amounts of Omega 6s (for example, corn oil) and the ratio is often 10:1. This can lead to arthritis, cancer and obesity in the general population and will also hamper recovery after exercise for cyclists, so look for ways to increase Omega 3s and decrease Omega 6s in your diet.

  Mono-unsaturated fats These are the best of all, and perhaps the most obvious source is olive oil. Simply increasing mono-unsaturated fat in the diet has been shown to lower weight without the need to consume fewer calories. They also protect your heart by lowering harmful cholesterol levels. There's even better news for cyclists because Omega 9 can also reduce inflammation of muscles and joints and responds well to exercise, which encourages it to continue burning after a ride, rather than adding to our fat stores.

TIP

One word of caution before you tip half a bottle of olive oil over your salad and expect miracles – it does still contain calories, so don't overdo it!

OTHER NUTRIENTS

The general recommendation for a healthy diet set by the World Health Organisation is five portions of fruit and vegetables a day. This is considered the level that will provide adequate levels of antioxidants and the other vitamins, minerals and nutrients required to reduce the risk of ill health. If you're exercising heavily, then you can expect to have a higher requirement, but if you're sticking to a pattern of healthy eating anyway, then the extra food you eat to take care of increased energy needs should also give you an above-average intake of vitamins and minerals.

Whether or not dietary sources are sufficient if you're putting your body through considerable training stress is another debate which hasn't yet produced a definitive answer. There are plenty of supplement companies with a large range of products and research papers which suggest there are benefits to using them. Some just cater for an increased need for regular vitamins, others are ergogenic aids, which claim, in particular, to help sports performance. Supplements are available to ensure an adequate intake of essential vitamins and minerals to maintain joint health and promote immune function. Some are also aimed at improving sporting performance by enhancing energy supply, delaying fatigue and promoting recovery.

Antioxidants

Hard exercise increases oxygen use in the muscles, and this in turn creates 'free radicals', which are known to damage body cells. Free radicals can, however, be neutralised by antioxidants such as Vitamins A, C and E. There has been some research to show that supplementing with both Vitamin C and E can indeed reduce muscle damage and speed up recovery, as well as protecting the immune system. Antioxidants work together rather than individually, so seeking to increase your intake from natural foods (such as highly coloured fruits and vegetables) is ideal. Taking 250ml of vitamin C daily will ensure maximum levels; any excess will be excreted in urine.

Antioxidant supplements often also contain selenium. This can also be found naturally in white fish, chicken, sunflower seeds and Brazil nuts.

Food	Portion size	Calcium content (milligrams)
Cheddar cheese	100g	720
Sardines	100g	380
Sesame seeds	100g	420
Milk	200ml	250
Soya milk	200ml	220
Chickpeas	100g	160
Spinach	100g	136
Tofu	100g	130
Wholemeal bread	100g	54
Broccoli	100g	47
Oranges	100g	40

Calcium

Virtually all the calcium in our bodies is in our bones (99 per cent), but it doesn't stay there. It acts as a reservoir for calcium, so if you don't eat enough then your bone density will be depleted. The other 1 per cent of calcium has a vital role in a number of functions, including the mechanism that makes our muscles work, so without calcium, exercise would be impossible. There is evidence that it could also play a role in energy metabolism and therefore help reduce body fat and prevent weight gain.

Calcium uptake requires zinc, and in turn it can inhibit the body's ability to absorb some types of iron. It's therefore best to get it from wholefood sources if possible.

Iron

Iron is very important for endurance exercise, and it's one of the nutrients often found to be low in people training regularly, especially women. It's a component of the red blood cells, which carry oxygen to the muscles, so if your iron levels are depleted you can expect to be weak and tired. Even if your levels aren't low enough for you to be anaemic, they will still have a significant effect on your performance. Heavy exercise programmes will in themselves cause iron loss, and for some women, heavy periods could see monthly losses of more than 50mg. Other factors could also affect iron levels, such as drinking tea or coffee, which both interfere with iron absorption.

The most readily available sources of dietary iron are animal products, especially red meat. If you're a vegetarian or vegan, or only eat white meat, then you have to take additional care to ensure you have an adequate intake of iron. Surprisingly, even cooking in a steel pan (without a non-stick coating) can add iron to your diet, and drinking orange juice with a meal will help too, as Vitamin C helps with the absorption of iron, especially that found in dark green leafy vegetables and beans. There are plenty of foods that are fortified with iron, such as breakfast cereals, but if you feel you are deficient, then consider a supplement and possibly visit your doctor for an accurate test.

Zinc

Zinc is another metal with an important role for active people, and since it competes for absorption with iron, if you need to supplement both, don't do so at the same time of day. Exercise increases the body's use of zinc, leading to the suggestion that athletes may need to increase their zinc intake. It is required for immune function and wound healing, so also plays a part in recovery. It can help to alleviate symptoms of a cold, and some research suggests that it can also improve aerobic performance.

Zinc deficiency is quite common amongst men, so consider supplementation or ensure an adequate dietary intake from green vegetables, and from many high-protein sources such as nuts, lentils, chicken and mussels.

Glucosamine and chondroitin

Glucosamine is a sugar that is made within the body to aid the growth of cartilage and keep tendons and ligaments healthy. Unfortunately, our production of glucosamine falls off with age, and relatively little is available from normal dietary sources. Hard exercise increases wear and tear on joints and tendons, so older riders may find they benefit from supplementing with glucosamine. Supplementation has another effect: greater use of another sugar, chondroitin, which has the job of keeping cartilage hydrated. Although some research has found positive effects with an intake of 520mg of glucosamine and 300mg of chondroitin a day, and there are also many supportive anecdotal reports, a major US study found no evidence to support these claims.

Creatine

If you look back to the section on energy pathways, you'll recall that creatine phosphate can be used to produce short bursts (less than 10 seconds) of anaerobic exercise. Its rapid synthesis for intense exercise makes it a perfect ergogenic aid for sprinters, but what use would it be for endurance athletes? That topic has been debated hotly since creatine became a popular supplement for explosive exercise events during the 1990s.

There is some evidence that taking a creatine supplement can provide benefits for cyclists during training by allowing higher-quality interval sessions. There is also a downside to its use, however: it may make you stronger but it will also make you heavier, since it encourages water retention and therefore weight gain. You can largely avoid this by supplementing in small doses, just sprinkling half a gram on food six times a day. This should prove beneficial for endurance cyclists at times when high intensities of energy use are also incorporated into their riding, and may be of particular interest to vegetarians, since the natural dietary source of creatine is steak.

Caffeine

One of the most effective ergogenic aids for cyclists is caffeine. It has a number of proven beneficial effects, and indeed at one time was on the list of banned substances. Now it's entirely legal and can help burn more fat, improve performance, lower perceptions of effort and reduce pain! It will also make you mentally sharper and more alert and so can aid motivation.

Before you head straight for the coffee jar there are a couple of other factors to note. First, the body does get used to caffeine, and therefore it's best not to use it regularly but save it for moments when you really need the help. Secondly, while your morning cup of coffee does contain significant amounts of caffeine, other substances in coffee interfere with its effects; it's therefore better to use caffeinated sports drinks or gels. Many racers use flat cola drinks in the final stages of races for a burst of caffeine and high-GI carbohydrates.

SLEEP

Alcohol

On the subject of popular drinks, you may wish to approach with caution those containing alcohol. There are many persuasive arguments for keeping alcohol consumption to a minimum, especially for competitive cyclists, and it may well be worth saving your drinking for periods when your riding load is low.

From an exercise point of view, alcohol is a disaster. It heads straight for the bloodstream, where it must be metabolised before the body uses other preferred fuel sources. In fact for several hours it reduces the body's ability to burn fat by more than 70 per cent. It also causes the body to lose water, increasing the risk of dehydration. Alcohol also increases levels of cortisol, a hormone that breaks down muscle tissue, and more bad news for muscle is that it also reduces the production of testosterone, which is a key factor in post-exercise recovery. Since this effect peaks immediately after exercise, an après-ride drinking session is best avoided.

Alcohol's other big payload is its calorie content (175kcal in 25ml), and since it increases appetite and lowers willpower, it can quickly lead to more fat deposits and weight increase. Even the day after drinking alcohol, fat metabolism will be down, and temperature control, reflexes and perception will still be affected, not least because alcohol also interferes with sleep patterns.

If you want a free, easy performance booster, you may need to look no further than your bed. Sleep deficit seems to be becoming an increasing problem for the general population. It quickly leads to poor concentration, while long-term sleep deficit can play a part in various health problems, including weight gain, cardiovascular disease and depression.

There's also growing evidence that in athletes even relatively small shortfalls of sleep, once accumulated, can affect performance. In fact it's a two-way street because intense exercise can often lead to disrupted sleep patterns due, for example, to 'restless leg syndrome'. It's not just the amount of sleep you have that is important either, but also the quality, so it pays to take steps to ensure you have lengthy undisturbed sleep. Keep a record of it in your training diary and try adding an extra hour a night for a week or two and see how it affects your performance.

In order to maximise sleep, consider the following.
- Make sure you're not hungry before going to bed but don't eat a large meal close to bedtime.
- Caffeine will affect your ability to fall asleep, and alcohol may lead to disturbance during the night, so avoid both for at least three hours before bedtime.
- Try to get some calm rest time before going to bed in order to wind down, and sleep in a cool, quiet room.
- Try increasing magnesium intake through supplements or foods such as pulses, nuts and wholegrain cereals.

THINKING ABOUT IT

Quiet relaxing time may provide a good opportunity to practise another element of improving cycling performance, and enjoyment. If you look at successful sportsmen and sportswomen, business people or even explorers, you'll find the majority have one particular attribute in common: mental toughness and a positive outlook.

WHEN THE GOING GETS TOUGH

Whether you're competing, taking part in a tough challenge ride, or just trying to get through a difficult training session, the right attitude can make a big difference to how well you succeed.

Even if you don't automatically have good emotional responses to challenges, it's possible to change your mental approach. This can be done using two techniques: imagery and self-talk.

- **Imagery** can be used to review or preview events and improve your emotional responses. It's important to visualise as authentically and as vibrantly as possible, so hear, feel and smell, as well as picture the exact scene. Now imagine the toughest moments. Feel how hard it is, how tired or in pain you could possibly be. Now imagine yourself coping with the situation, and being successful. Visualise yourself feeling empowered, reaching your goal, making the sprint, winning the race.
- **Self-talk** is a strategy for controlling emotions during an event. At difficult times your inner voice can become negative, questioning your ability and even talking you out of keeping going. So let's turn that into positive self-talk. As you get tired, the voice may say 'My legs are finished, I can't go on.' It's a message that will lead to failure, so let's change it. Tiredness tends to come and go during a ride, so turn the first part of the message into: 'My legs are tired right now.' Next consider a different response. A good technique for combating fatigue while riding is to take the focus off the pain and shift it to an element over which you do have control, such as pedalling. You now have a positive statement: 'My legs are tired right now, so I'll concentrate on my technique to pedal more efficiently.' This is far more likely to lead to success.

SEEING SUCCESS

Imagery can also be used to rehearse options during a race so that if the circumstance arises you are more likely to make the right decision. If you run the correct strategy or skill through your mind repeatedly, you're more likely to get it right when it counts. Use your training time to visualise your performance in your target event. Remember to include as much sensory awareness as possible, make it really vivid, make sure you see yourself in control and visualise a successful outcome.

FACT

It is estimated that 800 million bikes are in use throughout the world – twice the number of cars in existence.

SETTING GOALS

Research shows that setting goals leads to better performance. It appears to focus our attention and, providing we achieve our goals, it boosts our confidence. Goals are therefore useful both in reaching a desired level and in providing on-going motivation. In order to work successfully, however, the goals you set need to be thought out carefully. Goals can be categorised into short-, medium- and long-term targets.

- **Dream goals** are aspirational and should be difficult targets, which may take several years to achieve. They are the ultimate motivation for our efforts.
- **Mid-term goals** will be measured over months. They are milestones along the way towards long-term targets and are designed to track progress.
- **Short-term goals** may be quite basic, but they are also the most important. They are the aim of each and every training session or weekly block, and it's achieving each of these small steps that leads to success.

In order to set targets that will challenge, motivate and lead to steady progression, set SMARTER goals:

Specific
The more specific the better. Indicate precisely what is to be done.

Measurable
In order to measure success you should be able to quantify your goals accurately.

Attainable
Goals must be realistic and attainable, but also worthwhile and challenging.

Recorded
Write your goals down so that you have a contract with yourself.

Time-based
Set specific time limits.

Exciting
They will motivate you more than bland, boring targets.

Reversible
If you do fail to achieve your goals because of uncontrollable factors, don't let it dishearten you. For instance, in the event of injury, reset your goals accordingly.

INJURY AND ILLNESS

Riding your bike regularly will make you fitter and healthier. On the other hand, training hard will put pressure on your muscles and joints as well as your immune system, and you may well have to cope with illness or injury at some time. The best strategy for both is, of course, prevention, but if problems do occur, make sure you respond appropriately to ensure a quick and full recovery.

You are likely to face two types of injury: those caused by over-use or poor bike set-up, and those due to accidents.

USING YOUR BIKE AND BODY CORRECTLY

The first type of injury comes from over-use of your body or poor bike set-up, and commonly include neck and back pain or knee problems. Refer back to chapter 1 or get advice from a good bike shop to make sure your frame and stem are correctly sized, and that saddle and handlebars are set in the correct position. Take special care with your pedal set-up. Large forces are repeatedly put through the knee up to six thousand times an hour (with a cadence of 100rpm), so it's not surprising that incorrect load distribution can lead to inflammation and other injuries.

In addition to setting up your bike correctly, make sure you don't push your body too far or too fast too quickly; over-training is a quick short cut to injury problems. Make sure you follow nutritional guidelines for good muscle, joint and bone health, and include stretching in your training plan (see chapter 8). Good flexibility will help you to avoid over-use and postural injuries.

If you do suffer problems, don't ignore them. If you begin to get a pain, try to understand the cause. Stop riding, and if the pain persists and the area feels hot and tender, then RICE it:

Rest it
A few days off is better than causing a far more serious injury.

Ice it
Use an icepack or a bag of frozen peas wrapped in a tea-towel.

Compression
Reduce blood flow and swelling with firm support.

Elevate
If possible, keep the injury above your heart.

If the problem persists, see a sports physiotherapist. Make sure not only that the injury heals but also that you modify your position or training to avoid a repeat.

TIP

If you do have to take time off because of illness or injury, don't rush straight back to the same point in your training plan. Depending on the length of your lay-off, allow a few days to get up to speed and then start at the beginning of the last full week you completed on your training plan.

TIP
If you have damaged your helmet in a fall, make sure you replace it.

TRAUMA

The second category of injuries to consider is those from trauma. Falls and crashes may leave you with nothing more than damaged pride; more rarely they can lead to fractured bones. Prevention starts with ensuring your bike is in good working order and improving your handling skills. Make sure that you pay full attention to road or trail conditions at all times, and if you're riding with others, keep alert to stay out of trouble. Refer back to chapters 3 and 4 for more advice on riding skills.

If you're unlucky enough to sustain serious injury, you will need medical help and professional advice about what exercise you can continue to do. You may have heard stories of professional riders continuing to race with fractured collar bones or broken ribs, but they will only do so under close medical supervision. Even if you need an operation it may be that you can do some exercise quite soon afterwards, as long as you don't put any stress on the healing bone. Don't rush things, however, and remember to rewind your training schedule.

If your injuries from a fall are less serious you can deal with them yourself. First, make absolutely sure that you know what the damage is. You may initially only appear to have some surface bruising but there may be hidden damage to bones, joints or muscle. Also, check your bike to see that it has not been damaged before remounting. At the earliest opportunity, make sure you clean and if necessary dress any wounds. Try to keep the injured limb moving frequently if you can, to avoid it stiffening up too much, and drink plenty of fluids.

TIP
Carry a basic first-aid kit at all times so that you can deal with minor injuries on the spot.

Cycling is not an intrinsically dangerous activity, but don't forget that if you are involved in an encounter with a motor vehicle, the odds are heavily weighted against you (literally). To minimise the chances of such an eventuality:

- Make sure that other road users can easily see you – wear brightly coloured clothing or a high-visibility vest.
- Keep alert and anticipate what drivers may be about to do (don't assume they will always signal their intensions), especially in heavy traffic.
- Don't ride recklessly.
- Be ready to take evasive action if danger looms.

ROAD RASH

When falling off your bike you will often slide along the ground, taking off the top layers of skin. This can happen even without tearing clothing layers, but if the area is exposed, dirt and gravel will stick to the damaged tissue. This is road rash. Keeping wounds clean is one of the main reasons professional cyclists have shaved legs; the other being to avoid irritation from sports massage.

COLDS AND VIRUSES

One unwanted side-effect of training hard is suppression of the immune system. If you are over-training this can become a long-term state; under sustainable training regimes the effect may last for only an hour or for up to a day after a particularly arduous session. It's therefore sensible to take whatever precautions you can during the post-exercise period to minimise your contact with viruses until your immune system is back up to full strength.

- If possible, avoid contact with too many people, especially with anyone you know to have a cold.
- Don't share drink bottles, but do make sure you take on board adequate fluids and have good carbohydrate levels.
- Cultivate good hygiene practices, including frequent hand-washing.
- Eat a healthy diet and get plenty of sleep.

If you do get ill, should you train? If you feel weak or feverish the answer is a definite 'no'. If you have any aches, pains or other symptoms below the neck you should not be riding. On the other hand, if the symptoms are above the neck, such as runny eyes or a bunged-up nose, then you can still ride as long as you take it easy, and are prepared to return home promptly if your symptoms worsen. In fact you may well find that light to moderate exercise will sometimes ease the symptoms of a cold and make you feel much better.

If you do have a cold, then 'blue-level' rides (see p. 73) of 30–60 minutes will keep you ticking over until all your symptoms have gone and you're ready to resume full training. Don't be tempted to ride hard again too soon. It may be frustrating to have a setback to your training plan, especially if you have a particular goal around the corner. However, the closer the goal the more cautious should be your response to the illness. Returning to a full training regime before all the symptoms have gone may postpone a full recovery and could even lead to far more serious consequences, including post-viral fatigue. This can affect you mentally and physically for months afterwards, and doesn't seem to respond to rest.

The correct time to return to full riding after illness is once all your symptoms have gone. Even then, take a couple of days to gradually work back up to your normal training loads and then, as after injury, resume your plan at the beginning of the last full week you completed.

SADDLE SORES

A saddle sore may be a small problem but they've been enough to deny victory to great cycling champions, and can ruin your riding enjoyment.

They start as small lumps around the buttocks and groin area and if left untreated can become cysts or abscesses requiring surgical attention. They are caused by bacteria getting into the skin through abrasions or hair follicles, so one of the first preventative treatments is good hygiene. Always start a ride with clean shorts, and find a comfortable insert that doesn't cause chafing. Further protection can be applied with an anti-bacterial chamois cream which also acts as a lubricant to avoid friction.

TIP

It's also important to find a comfortable saddle (see p. 22). What works for one rider won't for another, so experiment and don't buy if you can't try!

OVER-TRAINING

Cyclists can be very competitive and very determined people. You want to succeed and you know that to do so you have to work hard, and sometimes that includes suffering. It can be the perfect attitude for achievement, but if you're not careful it can be the recipe for over-training.

How do you know if you're overdoing it? Keep an eye on some of these factors, and if too many crop up, and there's no other obvious explanation, it may be time to give yourself a break.

- Have you stopped looking forward to riding?
- Are you relieved when your session is over?
- Have you become more prone to illness?
- Is your morning resting heart rate 5–10 bpm higher than normal?
- Are you sleeping substantially more or less than normal?
- Have you lost your appetite?
- Have you lost a lot of weight?
- Are your legs constantly aching and tired?
- Are you moody and irritable?

Over-training is often caused by fear – fear that if you don't train you'll lose fitness or fall behind your rivals. To reframe your approach, analyse the evidence rationally. If you're working too hard without enough recovery your efforts will be counter-productive. If this continues, not only will your performances suffer but you may lose the appetite for cycling altogether, so ease up, and once you've recovered your freshness stick to a sustainable plan.

It's also important to ensure that cycling fits into your life, but doesn't become your life. Unless you're a professional rider, you will have a job and possibly a family to consider. Bike riding can be very time intensive but if your work and relationships suffer because of it then you need to reconsider your bike–life balance; after all, you will probably need family and friends to be on your side when it comes to your hobby if you want to get maximum enjoyment and achieve your goals.

FACT

A rider in the Tour de France may use upwards of 9000 calories a day and more than 100,000 over the three weeks. That's the equivalent of 150 burgers or 26 Mars bars a day.

PART THREE

CHALLENGE YOURSELF

Cycling provides many benefits, and also plenty of opportunities. Having worked through bike and body basics, the next thing to do is ask: where is it going to take you? As one of the 'greenest' inventions ever, it's perfect for the eco-conscious who see it as their contribution to saving the planet. If you want to see the world, what better way than by being a part of it rather than jetting in and jetting out of a tourist destination? Or how about conquering mountains and routes in the growing number of challenge rides around the world? And if you really have the competitive spirit, why not take on an 'all-comers' event and see just how fast you can ride?

In this section of the book we'll look at commuting, touring and Sportive riding, as well as racing. Whatever the challenge, let's accept it!

10: RIDING TO SAVE THE WORLD: COMMUTING

With so much talk of global warming, increased traffic congestion and rising fuel prices, it's no wonder a growing number of people want to make their daily journeys by bike. Riding to and from work can not only help to save the planet, but could also save you time and will almost certainly save you money. In three months the average car commuter can easily spend enough on fuel alone to buy a perfectly acceptable city bike. They may also spend hours every week just sitting in traffic jams making very slow progress. As long as you ride safely, especially in cities with a progressive cycling infrastructure, you may often find that getting to and from work is quicker and more enjoyable than going by car.

If you're following a training plan to build up to touring, Sportive riding or racing, then why not incorporate commuting into your weekly exercise schedule? You should at any rate include the mileage you are doing back and forth to work in your totals for the week, but consider on a couple of days taking a longer route home. You may well find that riding from stop light to stop light and out-sprinting traffic makes for very good interval training!

Of course, there are practical considerations. If the journey is a long one, maybe with hills, or you like to do it at a good pace, you may need to have showers at work. Some companies already provide these, along with secure cycle parking, and some countries even have tax schemes to encourage businesses to promote bike-friendly policies for their employees. In fact, some governments and employers provide grants or tax relief towards the cost of the bike itself. Find out from your human resources department, your local council office or national tax agency. If your company hasn't yet introduced facilities for cyclists, then let them know what they could do for you and how it might benefit them if more of their employees cycled to work.

TIP

Travelling by bike doesn't have to mean travelling alone. If you need to transport small children, there are a number of options. Very small children can be carried in a child seat mounted at the front of the bike. As they grow, a seat over the rear wheel will be more appropriate; these often slide over a rear rack, allowing quick and easy fitting and removal. Take care when you first ride with a child as you will have to get used to how the balance of the bike is affected.

An increasingly popular alternative is a trailer attached to the rear of your bike, or as the children get older, a tag-along bike. This is like a normal child's bike, but instead of a front wheel it attaches to your frame so that the child remains under your control.

If you have to travel to work by train, consider cycling at either end of your journey. Although you won't be very popular if you try to take a full-sized bike on a crowded commuter train (and many train companies operate restrictions on when bikes can be carried), a folding bike could be the ideal solution. These can be safely stowed in a smaller space than many suitcases. You will receive envious looks as you quickly unfold your bike and pedal off to work while your fellow passengers queue for a bus or crowded underground train.

GETTING EQUIPPED

Unless you want to ride in your work clothes, you'll need a way of transporting these. A backpack or panniers can do the job, but if you have a formal dress code at work, keeping your clothes un-creased could be a problem. One solution would be to drive to work one day of the week and drop off your clothes, bringing home last week's shirts/blouses on the return journey. This, of course, depends on having somewhere to store your clothes and having a good supply of shirts!

How to carry clothes and documents you need for work partly depends on the type of bike you ride. Any style of bike can be used for commuting but you can buy models designed especially for the job. For a more detailed discussion on choosing a bike, see chapter 1.

Some commuter bikes feature internal hub gears. These are an ideal choice for low maintenance. A fixed-gear bike will have similar benefits but this may not be suitable if your route is hilly.

If your bike doesn't have an integrated carrier, invest in a good-quality courier-style bag which will be comfortable to carry and will keep your clothes, papers, etc. clean, dry and safe.

Lights are very important unless you only commute in the summer. Get the brightest lights you can afford, and if possible they should be fairly light and easy to remove when leaving your bike. An alternative is a dynamo system (see p. 60).

Carry at least one lock and make it the biggest and strongest you can if you have to leave your bike in public or unsecured parking. If necessary, remove wheels and lock them to the frame and also take with you any quick-release parts (such as the saddle). However good your lock, there is still the possibility that your bike could be stolen, so make sure it's properly insured, either through your house insurance or through a cycling organisation.

Look back at chapters 2 and 6 for a more detailed discussion about additional equipment you could consider buying.

TIP

Carry a spare bungee with you to enable you to carry home piles of extra work or an unexpected purchase.

THE CITY COMMUTER BIKE
Straight handlebars in an upright position

26" (66cm – mountain bike size) wheels with slick tyres

Integrated carrier

Mudguards

Lights

Lock

You may also want to consider front shock absorbers if you ride over a route with lots of pot-holes.

STAYING SAFE: CYCLING TECHNIQUES

When cycling, obey all the rules of the road, including traffic lights and one-way streets, and don't ride on pavements. Try to think like a car driver to anticipate what drivers may do. Be confident and assertive of your right to be on the road, use hand signals where appropriate to inform others, and make eye contact to confirm you've been seen. If motorists give way to you, smile, nod or wave a thank you, and if you are ever met with aggression then remain calm.

Overtaking slow-moving or stationary traffic is fine if the conditions are suitable, but always be alert for sudden movements by vehicles or pedestrians, and beware of opening car doors. Don't be tempted to weave in and out of traffic and remember that drivers will have blind spots, especially those driving large vehicles. Take particular care at junctions.

If you've been used to travelling to and from work by car, you may wish to re-plan your journey. The obvious route to travel by car may not be the best route by bike, especially if you're apprehensive about cycling on busy roads. You may find a shorter or quieter route using side roads or cycle paths, and more attractive scenery if you can travel through parks or along riverbanks. Consider trying out the route before you start using it to commute, and on your first day give yourself plenty of time.

Hopefully you'll find that after riding to work you'll be in a much more energised and happier frame of mind for the day ahead. And once you've got used to using your bike for these short journeys, consider expanding your horizon. Why not make that trip to friends or family in the next town by bike too, and then why not plan a weekend round trip or a whole holiday!

TIP

Your local council or cycling organisation will probably have maps or books showing designated and recommended cycle routes and usually highlighting traffic-free sections. In the UK, the National Cycle Network has established thousands of miles of routes within and between most towns and cities.

11: RIDING TO SEE THE WORLD: TOURING

Riding my bike is work for me, and it's serious. But that doesn't mean I don't still enjoy riding for fun. I was lucky enough to grow up in a beautiful part of Wales, and since then have lived in Italy and Switzerland. Although much of my riding is training-specific, I do still have time to just take in the scenery and visit new places. This is where my cycling began, on family touring holidays, and I hope I'll have many more when my professional career is over.

Touring may mean venturing a little way from home for a weekend away, a two-week trip (maybe to another country), or perhaps a major trek around the globe.

BE PREPARED!

Having the proper equipment, making sure you're fit enough and planning the trip properly will all help ensure it goes successfully. There is a certain excitement and sense of freedom about just getting on your bike and seeing where you end up. It's a shame to lose such spontaneity, but in many cases it's sensible to decide in advance what type of ride or tour you wish to do. This can depend on the region where you plan to ride, the terrain you expect or wish to find, the distance you intend to cover, the climate or seasonal conditions, and any places of interest you wish to stop at or visit.

Whether it's a weekend trip where you stay overnight and ride back the next day, a cycling holiday based in one location with different routes each day, or a tour through a whole region carrying all your supplies, planning will help to ensure it goes smoothly.

YOUR BIKE AND EQUIPMENT

First, check the condition of your bike and its equipment and make any repairs in advance. If you have the option of changing gear ratios, choose an appropriate range depending on whether you will be riding on the flat or in a hilly area. If you have plenty to carry, a fully laden bike will require a smaller gear to ride comfortably on climbs, and will also take more stopping, so check your braking performance too. (See p. 130 for advice on loading your bike.)

Although racing frames use a variety of sometimes exotic materials, many tourers are still built using steel because of its comfort, strength and longevity (see chapter 1). Traditionally

THE TRADITIONAL TOURING BIKE

Road bike with carriers for panniers
Narrow tyres
Dropped handlebars (more responsive and better for riding at speed)
Bar-end gear changers
Option to carry 'light' luggage
Wide selection of gears

cantilever brakes give the extra stopping power required for a heavy bike when fully laden, but you can also get an even more powerful option. Hydraulic systems provide outstanding braking performance, but may pose a repair problem if your route is particularly far flung!

Compared with a training ride, you're quite likely to make several stops, possibly leaving the bike unattended while you eat or explore a place of interest. You should therefore always carry a suitable lock (see chapter 6).

PREPARE YOURSELF: TRAINING FOR THE TRIP

You'll need to be fit enough for your chosen tour, so take that into account when planning a trip. If you intend to ride sixty miles or more a day for ten days, you must train yourself to do that comfortably. The last thing you want to do on a holiday is struggle so much that you can't enjoy the scenery and the places you visit. Adapt the training plans from chapter 7 so that you're confident of riding day after day, completing the time or distances required, and also coping with the terrain involved.

TIP

When training for a tour, practise riding with the bike fully laden sometimes if you intend to carry luggage. Carrying extra weight will mean more effort is required, and you also need to get used to the handling characteristics of a tour bike with full panniers (see p. 130).

PLANNING THE ROUTE

Traditionally, cycle tourists would carry a map to help them follow their route, either making stops to check directions or perhaps keeping it in a plastic pouch on top of a handlebar-mounted bag. This is still a cheap and perfectly functional method, but with the availability of GPS systems for cyclists, you can be directed by a satellite navigation system in the same way as many drivers. You can also make notes on a small card or name the important landmarks so you do not have to carry a big tourist guide or map. If possible, have your notecard laminated or put it in a small plastic holder and carry it in a jersey pocket.

If you plan your route on a map of an unfamiliar area, remember that the shortest route between two places is sometimes the steepest! Books, magazines and websites publish recommend routes and in many countries there are networks of signposted cycle routes. If you can use these recommended routes, then this will help you to know what to expect in advance. Bike paths or cycle routes usually offer a much better alternative to riding on busy roads; most towns now have some cycle provision in their transport planning. You may also find bike routes through some parks, which can be good short cuts.

Ideally you should leave some slack in your timetable to allow you the flexibility to stop at some places longer than expected or to deal with emergencies such as punctures during the ride, and remember to allow time for re-fuelling.

TIP

Credit cards are lightweight and worth carrying in your back pocket in case of unexpected events!

CLOTHING

As well as making sure your bike is properly kitted out, also think of what you'll need for the trip. Clothing needs to be appropriate for the conditions. If you intend to have long days in the saddle, remember it could be cold in the early mornings and evenings, but much warmer in the middle of the day. Similarly, it might be very warm in a sunny valley, but quite chilly on mountains, especially when it comes to descending hills. Consider, therefore, having layers that you can remove or replace as appropriate (see chapter 2), and make sure you have enough room in bags or pockets to stow them when you take them off.

Weather can easily change, especially in the hills, so if there is any chance of rain, you'll need waterproofs with you. Few things will make you more uncomfortable than getting soaked to the skin if you don't have the right clothes. If it is wet, put on your rain jacket and any extra layers straight away. It's much better to be too warm and take layers off later than to get cold and suffer because of it. With the right clothing, you'll find riding in the rain is not as bad as it may seem at first!

TIP

Put on an extra layer or wind-block jacket before long descents, which can feel very cold because of the chill factor as you pick up speed downhill, especially if you're damp with sweat from the climb. If you don't want to carry extra jerseys, you can buy or ask for some newspapers to stick inside your jersey and protect your chest. They make great wind stoppers to prevent you getting chilled!

Of course moisture can come from inside as well as out, so if you intend on stopping, it could be worth carrying a spare under-vest to change into so that you don't have your sweaty clothes close to your skin.

Hopefully the sun will shine on your riding sometimes, but that can bring its own problems too. Remember to take sun block and perhaps something to cover your neck. You'll also need to increase your fluid intake if you're riding under a strong sun. Consider planning your trip so that you can avoid riding during the middle of the day when the sun is at its hottest.

LOADING YOUR BIKE

The more equipment and luggage you have, the more carefully you will have to pack your panniers, including making sure you only take what you really need! Carrying things in a backpack may be fine for short journeys such as a daily commute, but for long journeys you'll soon find this quite uncomfortable; it's far better to let your bike carry the load. You can mount a bag on the handlebars, as well as on top of a rear rack, which will also support large panniers on either side. You can also have smaller panniers either side of the front wheel, attached to carriers mounted on your forks.

Weight distribution is very important to ensure stability. Steering is compromised if all the weight is on the back, and this can make for a very unnerving time when cornering at speed. The ideal ratio would be 60 per cent at the back, 40 per cent at the front, and also make sure it's evenly weighted on either side. The alternative solution is a trailer, but while this means you can carry more, it can also make the trip harder and limit you to certain routes.

Make sure you pack things you might need more frequently or in a hurry (such as waterproofs) in a separate pocket or at the top so you can get at them quickly and easily, and don't forget to take a few things to do when you're not riding, such as books, an mp3 player or hand-held game console.

TIP

It's worth leaving space, or even a whole empty pannier, to stock up with food at your destination and don't forget to pack some high-GI emergency snacks, such as an energy gel or dried fruit.

GETTING THERE AND STAYING THERE

The true cycling holiday would be a start-to-finish, home-and-back, entire trip on the bike. However, that won't be practical if your destination is some distance away, and possibly overseas.

It may be possible to hire bikes at your destination. This is a particularly good option if you're touring light, or combining riding with a sizeable off-bike element.

Remember to plan well ahead and research your options in advance to make sure you can guarantee getting an appropriate bike. You may wish to take your own pedals with you and you will of course need to take your own shoes and clothing. Consider what else you will need and what you may hire or buy locally; for example, bike bottles are cheap but bulky and normally easily available when you arrive.

If you're taking your own bike you have a choice of boat, train, plane and automobile! There are a variety of bike carriers for cars, either rear or roof mounted. Roof racks don't block access to your boot during your journey, but will have a bigger impact on fuel consumption and may take a little more effort to load. Don't forget there may be added costs or restrictions that may be applied by ferry companies if you have a sea crossing. Make sure you mount bikes to the rack very securely for safety, and include a lock for security if the car and bikes will be unattended.

TIP

If you're making the whole journey by bike you can still cross the water. Most ferry companies will carry cyclists quite cheaply.

TRAVELLING BY TRAIN

Bike and train should be a perfect combination for long-distance travel, but this isn't always the case. It varies from country to country, and even for different regions within countries. Some train companies won't carry bikes at all, or only at certain times. Other restrictions might mean only one or two bike places are available per train, which is not very helpful if you're travelling in a group of three or more! You may also be required to book in advance, and in some cases you can't travel with your bike, which may be carried on a completely different train! Thorough planning beforehand should help avoid problems, and it's a good idea to carry with you any written confirmation of regulations from the company in case individual staff try to make their own rules!

FLYING WITH A BIKE

The growth of cheap air travel in recent years has made the world a very small place. Environmental issues apart, this means you can feasibly tour on any continent of the world, and even ride in far-flung or exotic locations on a relatively short trip.

Just as with trains, you may find some flight operators more cycling friendly than others. Although you can dismantle your bike and pack it so that it's indistinguishable from other luggage, you should check individual airline policies beforehand. It's no good getting to the airport at the start of your holiday only to meet a total refusal to accept your bike on the plane.

If you've ever watched the way baggage handlers load and unload the hold, you'll be keen to pack your bike with as much protection as possible! You can either use the less bulky option of a bike bag, or alternatively a bigger, hard-case bike box. With both options, some dismantling will be required – removing wheels, bars, saddles, etc. This is not only necessary to fit everything in, but also reduces the risk of damage. Make sure the frame is well protected from possible knocks (pipe cladding is very effective) and place something in between the ends of forks and stays to avoid them being deformed if your bag is crushed.

Besides offering more protection, a bike box will also provide you with more stowage options. Clothing, helmet, shoes and other luggage can be placed in with the bike and carefully arranged to further cushion the frame, but make sure you cover any oily parts such as the chain.

If you intend setting off on tour directly from your destination airport, remember that you'll need safe storage for your bike bag or box. Once again a box can make a good option in this case, allowing you to stow your non-cycling travel clothes.

ACCOMMODATION

If you wish to travel light you can stay in hotels, eat in restaurants, and carry only a few clothes and a credit card! You might, however, want to be more self-sufficient and camp overnight, carrying all your luggage (including tents) with you. In either case, weigh up the options of planning and booking hotels, guest houses or campsites in advance for peace of mind, or the alternative of finding somewhere to stay as you go along. The latter approach will give you much more flexibility and you won't feel pressured to get to a certain location every day. However, you may also waste part of the day searching for a hostel or campsite, and may end up having to pay more for not having booked accommodation in advance.

TIP

If you do intend to camp, don't set off on a long tour for your first trip. Instead, have a short trial run, staying overnight close to home, to iron out any potential problems.

ON THE ROAD

Let someone know when you're setting off and what time you're expected to arrive. If you have a riding partner they can provide support in case of an accident, but if you're by yourself you should have a back-up plan in case something does go wrong. Carry your mobile phone with you or make sure you have small change or a phone card for public telephones. You should also carry your personal details where they are easy to find, including medical information and contact numbers.

If you're doing big mountain climbs, pace yourself! It's better to choose a steady pace within your capabilities for the first half of the climb, and then push on as you near the top, rather than start too hard and 'die'.

Pedalling on flat roads at a high cadence will move you along at a good speed and reduce the build-up of fatigue as the day goes on. Big gears and a low cadence can really tire your legs out quickly. On a touring holiday you will probably want to take things at a leisurely pace rather than racing from place to place, but it can still be physically demanding, especially if you're riding on consecutive days. It's important, therefore, that you have trained for the distances you intend to cover, and have at least some runs when you are fully laden to replicate the touring experience.

FUEL YOUR TRIP

Make sure you have enough fluid and food to fuel your trip, and have an idea of where you will be able to stop to refill bottles and restock pockets. Even if you're riding at a leisurely pace and not sweating as much as you might in a hard training session, you still need to keep well hydrated. A 10 per cent loss in fluid will result in more than a 30 per cent loss in performance.

During each day's ride, remember to eat little and often. Your energy supply needs to be like a constant conveyor belt; what you eat will be powering your legs in 20 minutes' time. If you forget to eat, your energy supply will stop! If you do 'blow', 'bonk' or 'hit the wall' (see p. 100), you will have over-reached your body's capabilities and feel you have absolutely no energy at all. If you have food with you, eat this straight away – the higher the sugar content, the better. In this situation, you will realise the importance of carrying high-GI emergency snacks. If necessary, stop to buy some food and look for something with a high sugar content.

If you find yourself in this position there is no easy solution for finishing the ride. You may decide to keep on going and slowly make your way to the end, hoping to recover a little as you go. If you have time, however, consider stopping. A good rest and time for your body to digest some food is a better option, so that you can start again with more energy. This is easier to do if you have been realistic about the distances you plan to cover, and the time you have given yourself to get from place to place.

TIP
Remember to drink even when it's raining! You may not feel hot but you will still sweat and will need to replace the lost fluids.

FACT
H.G. Wells said: 'When I see an adult on a bicycle, I have hope for the human race.'

DO YOUR RESEARCH

It's important when travelling, especially if you're visiting different cultures, to be aware of local customs – from practical things such as when shops may be shut, to whether certain dress codes or other behaviours are acceptable, and what potential pitfalls or dangers there may be.

It's therefore worth doing as much research as possible before your trip. In certain regions, travelling with organised groups or on trips arranged by an experienced specialist company might prove to be both more enjoyable and safer. They can also offer vehicle back-up support, which will take care of luggage and is ideal should there be any problems. These trips are often linked to charities so you can see the world, meet new people and raise money at the same time.

If you have a bike, the world really is there for you to see, as so many people have found. Plenty of cycle tourists have written down their experiences in informative and often highly entertaining accounts of their travels by bike. Read a few of them and they are sure to give you plenty of ideas and motivation for trips of your own, and if you wish to start by doing some online research there are plenty of great websites (see the resources section on pages 160–161).

12: RIDING TO CONQUER THE WORLD: SPORTIVES

There's something heroic about riding a bike, something that lends itself to the epic. Get together a group of committed cyclists and there'll be plenty of stories about how far or how fast they've ridden, and discussions about the steepest climb or the hardest day.

WHY SPORTIVES?

Let's be honest, there's at least a little part of many of us which in a strange way loves to suffer, and certainly likes to revel in the knowledge that we had to dig really deep inside us to prevail, but somehow managed to make it through! It's that desire to test limits that has seen a massive explosion in recent years of the 'Sportive'. This isn't a gentle leisure ride to admire the scenery, though usually there are plenty of stunning views to see. And it isn't a race, though some riders treat it as though it were. In many ways it's the essence of cycling: a moving community of like-minded people, both supporting and competing against each other at the same time. A Sportive is an event that riders of widely varying abilities can share and enjoy in their own different ways. It's a day when you challenge yourself to see just what you can do, and a ride that will provide a few more stories for cycling gatherings to come.

There's another inspirational aspect about cycling that few, if any, other sports can share. How many humble Sunday footballers can play in the world's famous stadiums, running on the same pitch as legends like Pelé or Beckham or Zidane? You can't just stroll up to Wimbledon or Flushing Meadows and play on the Centre Court and dream of being Martina Navratilova. But cyclists can ride the Ventoux and Alpe d'Huez. They can cover the exact route of a northern one-day classic, ride the roads where Merckx and Coppi played out their greatest days. You can even ride a stage of the Tour de France with closed roads and crowds and TV cameras, just days before the current pros sweep through at breathtaking speed. 'He won it in 4 hours 12; I managed to do it under 6 you know.' The Etape du Tour was one of the first Sportives and is still the most high profile: 9000 riders tackling the legendary climbs of the world's greatest cycle race. But there are many more; right around the globe, all through the year, big and small.

Riders have always challenged themselves. Point-to-point records go back to the earliest days of cycling, and in 1897 a group of Italian cyclists rode 200km between sunrise and sunset. They became known as 'Les Audacieux', which means bold and courageous. Long-distance Audax rides have continued ever since in several parts of the world. They can be anything up to 600km long and riders are left largely to their own devices. A Brevet card is provided which has to be stamped along the route as proof of completion.

But Audax rides have been quickly eclipsed by the Sportive. The key difference that has attracted so many riders seems to be the organisation that's involved. You can expect organisers to have made a careful choice of suitable roads, taking in the best riding and usually some very challenging climbs. The route will be well signposted and carefully marshalled. There will be feed stations at start and finish and at intervals along the route. Some events will be able to provide mechanical assistance and a 'broom wagon' to pick up any riders who find the experience tougher than they expected. Timing chips may also be available so you'll know exactly how long it took and, if it's important to you, where you finished. Following the lead of the Etape du Tour and Italian-style Gran Fondos, many Sportives provide medals based on your finishing time, challenging you to achieve Gold, Silver or Bronze.

Some sportivistes are racers who fancy a change, or sometimes riders who'd love to race but don't have the time to commit to a racer's training programme. For some the attraction is that they don't need to get a racing licence or join a national organisation, but can still get a very competitive ride. And they will. At the front of many a Sportive you would be hard pushed to know it wasn't a race. And all the way down the field you'll find little groups of friends, or people who have become friends on the day, competing with each other at their own level to get to the finish first.

TRAINING FOR A SPORTIVE

Remember, these rides are supposed to be challenging in both their distance and terrain. Make sure you train properly to reach the right level before entering. 180km in mountainous terrain might take a fit rider five hours, but could easily mean eight or nine hours in the saddle for others. Using the template of our training plans in chapter 7, steadily increase the hours of your long weekend ride so that you know you can cover a similar distance before the event.

SPORTIVE TECHNIQUES

Even if you're not intent on the pseudo-racing, those competitive little groups of riders can be a great help. Why not hitch a ride? After all, if you have 160km to ride, why not take advantage of the slipstream and make good time! There is a potential pitfall to this 'drafting' strategy. It's certainly worth pushing yourself a little harder than you might otherwise ride, if that keeps you in the shelter of a group, rather than the alternative of facing a long ride on your own into a headwind. However, if you're inexperienced it's easy to push yourself too hard to stay with a higher-level group, only to blow up completely, especially if you've over-done it before a major climb.

If you're not a speed freak, don't be put off by the hot pace at the front. There will be just as many riders aiming only to complete the distance and happy to ride at a steady speed. There are many friendships formed out on the road and you will often find other riders or other groups riding at a pace that's just right for you. Many Sportives offer alternative routes, perhaps half the distance or maybe routes avoiding the major climbs. Even if you plan to do the full ride you can change your mind en-route if you find the going too tough.

TAKING PART: CHOOSING YOUR EVENT

The popularity of many of the big events means that they can quickly become over-subscribed. If you plan to ride in an event, contact the organiser as soon as you can to find out when you can enter and whether or not places will sell out. If it's an event you really want to do, make sure you sign up early; there's no point training for months for a specific objective, only to discover that you can't take part.

Most events can be entered online, and top European Sportives have pages in English as well as their own language. You may be required to provide a medical certificate to confirm you're fit enough to ride. The growth in popularity of Sportives has even led to a world series sanctioned by the *Union Cycliste International* known as the 'Golden Bike'. There are plans for the Golden Bike to grow as more rides around the globe reach the specific standards that are necessary for inclusion, but with popularity increasing you should find local events too.

THE GOLDEN BIKE SERIES
- Cape Argus Pick'n'Pay Cycle Tour: South Africa (March)
- De Ronde van Vlaanderen: Belgium (April)
- Gran Fondo Internazionale Felice Gimondi: Italy (May)
- Quebrantahuesos: Spain (June)
- CycloSportive l'Ariégeoise: France (June)
- Gruyère Cycling Tour: Switzerland (August)
- Rothaus RiderMan: Germany (September)
- Wattyl Lake Taupo Cycle Challenge: New Zealand (November)

TIP

If you intend to ride several Sportives in the year, make sure you space them out to give yourself recovery time, until your fitness improves to the level where you can ride them more often.

How do you choose which Sportives to enter? Pick them according to what you're capable of, and when best suits you. There is no point entering an event that comes at a time of year when you know you will have been too busy to train fully. If you're travelling abroad, you could choose a ride that fits in with a longer holiday. You might opt for a specific ride because of the route it covers, or you might be attracted by the fact that some sign up big-name cyclists to be part of the field. The largest events will be very busy; with thousands of riders on the road at the start of events, it can be very slow for the first few kilometres until the field starts to spread out a bit. This is particularly frustrating if you're hoping for a good time but have a start some way towards the back of the field. If you do have a racing licence, then some events may give you preference for a good starting position.

WHAT DOES IT COST?

Entry fees vary widely for Sportives. Some Italian Gran Fondos, for instance, might cost £25. In the UK, some major rides charge £25 whereas another 2008 ride on fully closed roads had an entry fee of £49. The Etape du Tour is likely to set you back much more because many of the entries are only available from cycling holiday companies as complete packages, including travel and accommodation. It is, however, a very special event, with fully closed roads and entertainment.

Remember, however, that the Etape is a point-to-point event, so you'll need to arrange transport and not get caught with your car 150km away when you finish.

The advantage of entering the Etape with an organised company is that it can take care of details like that, along with other transport needs and hotels. If you're doing a big event on your own, try to book accommodation early because it can quickly get booked up. For travelling with your bike, follow the advice given in chapter 11, and don't forget to find an insurance policy that will cover you and your bike.

THE BIKE

Most riders in a Sportive will ride racing-style road bikes, but perhaps with a few modifications. Frame materials and geometry can be adjusted slightly to give a less sprightly bike than a typical racer, but provide more comfort for the long hours in the saddle. You won't need to take many extras with you, but a small saddle pack containing spare tubes and basic tools is an essential precaution. Just as in racing, you will usually be required to wear a helmet, and make sure you carry a range of layers and waterproofs, especially if you're riding in the mountains, where weather conditions can quickly change, even in the summer.

TIP

Be careful and don't take unnecessary risks; you want a day to remember and a tale to tell, but not a real horror story!

13:RIDING TO BEAT THE WORLD: RACING

To truly test yourself and pit your strength and skills against others, racing is the perfect outlet for your competitive spirit! I began cycling for fun with my family, but as soon as I learnt about races, the Tour de France and the Olympics, I was fascinated and wanted to know how I would match up against my rivals in a real race.

TIP
In most cases, if you want to race you'll need a licence. Contact the governing body for cycling in your country for details. Although you'll have to pay upfront costs, there are usually a number of benefits, including insurance.

The great thing about cycling is not only the range of different disciplines, but also the fact that almost anybody can race. There are categories for everyone, from young children to senior citizens, races for men and women, and event categories based on a wide range of abilities. So from Elite to 4th Cat Road Racer, Fun to Expert Mountain Biker, or from Junior to Veteran you can enjoy competitive racing against riders of a similar standard.

I found out about a local cycling club and races taking place in my area and did my first event, a cyclo-cross race on my steel mountain bike in the Under-12 category. I can still remember the nerves on the start line, but as soon as the starting gun went I was into my rhythm, going as fast as my legs would take me, negotiating the course to find the quickest way through the obstacles and chasing the rider in front with all my strength to try and move to a higher place. I finished exhausted, covered in mud but thrilled with the feeling of pushing myself to my limits and getting a result to reflect my efforts. I could already think how I wanted to improve my performance, how I wanted to get faster and how I wanted to win races and get a place on the podium! This is the racing bug; it had already captured me and since then I have been on a mission to try and achieve the best performances possible and win the biggest races in cycling.

There is so much variety in the sport of cycling, with different disciplines to choose from. These individual branches of the sport require different natural abilities so there is always an element of cycling for every cyclist to specialise in. I raced in all the disciplines while moving up through the age categories, mixing mountain biking with road racing, track racing and time trials. It gave me a great variety of skills and knowledge of different racing situations. However, as time went on I knew it was road racing that appealed to me most.

This chapter outlines the various cycling disciplines, the natural abilities and skills required for each and a guide to the tactics involved. If you're interested in racing, watch some races and then enter a few to find out for yourself what it's like. You can then specialise and develop your strengths, depending on what discipline suits you best.

ROAD RACING

This is often described as the 'King of Sports'. It is everything – your body, your mind and your bike are all important in this massed-start racing with the simple aim of finishing first.

There are one-day races, World Championships and the Olympic Games, World Cups and Classics, which test your power and strength in races of 3–4 hours for women, and 4–6+ hours for men. You need to have the power to change speed, attack, climb and sprint. You also need to be physically prepared for the terrain you will cover – anything from flat windy roads, to mountains and even cobbles. You need to be tactically ready to pit your strengths against your rivals' weaknesses and you need to select the right equipment, tyres and gear ratios for the day.

Then there are stage races, which can last for a few days or up to three weeks for the Grand Tours like the Tour de France, the Giro d'Italia and the Vuelta a Espagna. There are many winners in these races, with sub-categories for sprints and mountain primes, and prestige for the winner of each stage. The big prize, though, goes to the best all-round rider, the one with the range of consistent talent to become the overall winner by completing the whole course in the shortest time.

PHYSICAL SKILLS

Road racing has a team element, so you can pool your strengths against other teams to try and get the win for one of your riders. This introduces a big range of possible tactics. Depending on the race, teams usually have between four and nine riders, all of whom will have specific roles (see p. 144).

ROAD BIKE AND RIDER
Wheels – lightweight
Tyres/tubulars – lightweight, thin
Close gear ratios
Frame number clip
Frame – lightweight
Bottle cages
Bike computer/heart rate monitor
Race jerseys – pockets for food, rain jacket

LEADERS' JERSEYS

The most famous jersey in cycling is the Yellow Jersey awarded to the leader of the Tour de France. Other races and other categories within stage races also have jerseys for the leader of the competition. These make the rider easily recognisable within the peloton.

The Rainbow Jersey is very special as it's worn by the World Champion. The honour of having the blue, red, black, yellow and green bands around your chest lasts for every race for the next twelve months. After this time the jersey passes to the next winner, but former world champions are never forgotten; they are allowed to wear rainbow bands on the collars and sleeves of their jerseys for the rest of their careers.

Each nation also awards a National Champions jersey to the rider who wins the country's annual championship race, and as with the Rainbow Jersey, national champions wear the jersey for the whole season following their victory, with bands on collars and sleeves thereafter.

- **Domestiques** are able to support and deliver their leaders to the critical parts of the race in a good enough position and condition for the leader to put in their winning move. Almost every rider has to play the role of domestique at some time in their career, and along with closing gaps and launching attacks they may also have to pace their leader back to the bunch after a puncture or other mechanical problem, and sometimes even give them their bike! Other duties include sheltering their leader from the wind, collecting water bottles and carrying clothing for team mates. It's very satisfying to know that your efforts have help shaped the outcome of the race and allowed a rider from your team to win.
- **Climbers** have a fantastic power-to-weight ratio that really makes the difference on the climbs. Once the road goes up they are in their element and can launch attacks that will quickly leave non-climbers trailing a long way down the mountain.
- **Sprinters** are powerful riders with a big turn of speed. They have an inbuilt tactical sense of what to do and where to be in those physical and hectic moments at high speed as the peloton closes in on the finish line. They also have a fearless nature, battling for every inch when everybody wants to be in that one ideal position to unleash their sprint for victory.

TIP

You need to judge your effort to the line. If you go too soon you will die, as you cannot keep up the high speed for more than about 15 seconds. If you decide to follow another rider, you'll get shelter from the wind by riding in their slipstream, but be careful not to leave it too late to make your move as you may not have enough time to go past before the finish line. Judging which wheel to follow is also one of the key skills for a successful sprinter.

- **Team leaders** are riders with all the above skills – climbing, sprinting and keeping a close watch on their rivals – and they also have the ability to make split-second decisions that may change the outcome of the race. They are usually able to excel on all terrain and in all conditions.

Before a race it is good to think clearly and realistically about your strengths and those of your team, as well as your rivals' weaknesses, in relation to the course you will be riding. Use this to decide on a race strategy that will hopefully result in success for your team. There may be a team director who can give feedback on time gaps or changes in circumstances during the race. The director will also be able to update the riders if there is a change in tactics or strategy, and may be better placed to take a wider view or decide things more calmly than riders caught up in the heat of the moment during race development.

If you don't have a team director, a team captain may be appointed who is not necessarily the team leader, but is an experienced rider who can take charge at important moments and offer sensible and motivational words to help the team achieve the best they can.

TACTICAL SKILLS

Tactics are varied and almost anything goes in road racing. Generally you should aim to save as much energy as possible until you decide it's your moment to change the shape of the race and make your bid for glory. This could be marking your nearest challengers until a sprint finish, where you hope your speed will take you to victory. If your strength is climbing, you could attack before or on a hill, when your extra power will make the difference, and form a solo or group break-away. Sometimes it's necessary to put some energy and effort into splitting up the field before the finish to give you more options at the end of the race. So much depends on the course, the terrain, the wind and the type of finish, but the more you race the more you'll get a sense of the right option, so follow your instincts and learn through trial and error. This is especially true for timing. If you make your move a moment too soon, other riders may easily be able to follow you; on the other hand, if you delay too long it could give your rivals enough time to recover and be strong enough to chase you down!

Good skills to practise for road racing are attacks, closing or bridging a gap and, if you'll be racing as a team, some lead-outs and team break-aways.

The Peloton

Riding in a peloton, or bunch, can be daunting to begin with. You are totally surrounded by riders and any sudden movements by you or others could easily cause a crash. You must build up confidence in riding at speed close to others; start on training rides and then put it into practise in racing. Don't be afraid to call to other riders to let them know you're there in case they haven't realised it. If you have to touch other riders with your hands to defend your space and safety, or as you move past, do this with confidence and courtesy at the same time.

TIP

It's best to ride near the front of the bunch. You should still be sheltered from direct wind by the riders in front, but close enough to see any attacks or moves by your rivals and able to react immediately if necessary. You are also at greater risk of being held up by crashes if you're towards the back of the peloton.

A break-away

A break-away will normally start with an attack by one rider. Although solo efforts sometimes work, one rider is usually joined by a number of others. Whether this proves to be a successful move depends on whether the riders from different teams all feel it's in their interest for the break-away group to stay in front for the rest of the race. If this is the case, you should all try to cooperate and share the pace equally to keep the speed high, and also allow recovery after your turn at the front.

If the group is between two and five riders it's best to ride in a 'pace-line', where the leading rider puts in the effort to keep the speed up while the others follow closely behind, taking advantage of the slipstream effect (see p. 41). This keeps the 'group' speed higher than one a solo rider could maintain. If there are more than five, you can use a 'chain-gang', riding in two lines with riders moving up on one side, usually the side sheltered from the wind, to take a turn at the front. After completing a turn at the front, each rider moves over to the outside and the next rider moves past to take over the pace-making. Do not free-wheel back down the line, but take two easy pedal revolutions and then move behind the next rider once they have made their effort. This means less difference between the speed on the front and the speed on the back and you maintain a high speed with less fatigue for the riders involved.

As the end of the race gets closer, beware of attacks from within the group. You will all have to weigh up the threats from other riders. As the finish approaches, some riders may stop working, some may try to make attacks. Don't play into the hands of others by giving them a free opportunity, but remember that once the group stops co-operating, the chasing pack can quickly close you down.

The finish

As the finish gets closer you have to assess your chances of winning from a bunch or whether you need to try a solo effort. Once you've decided on your game plan you should try to save your energy until your moment comes. If you want to break away, think about attacking when another rider has just been caught, after the summit of a climb or when the pace starts to slow down. If you want to try and win the sprint, choose to follow a fast finisher or get a team mate to lead you out. With just under 200m to go you should accelerate with all your force, often called a 'kick' because of the explosive power you produce, and there is no easing off until you cross the line.

TIP

Practise lunging for the line by throwing your arms straight in front of you and pushing your butt behind the saddle to create a momentary spurt of momentum for the bike. It may make you cross the line a couple of centimetres ahead, and with photo-finish equipment it may mean the difference between winning the race and finishing second, or being on the podium or not.

TIME TRIALS

TRAINING

Tactics and skills are a key part to road racing, but you'll get nowhere without good physical condition. Professional racers train 20 hours a week or more. An amateur with other commitments may not be able to manage that, but you can adapt the training plans from chapter 7 to improve your performance at functional threshold and develop the power required for breaks and sprints.

If you're able to increase your training, consider trying to fit in 15 hours. If you had already reached the 12-hour schedule from chapter 7, the 15-hour plan (see opposite) increases the hours and adds in a little more racing specificity to your training.

Once you've reached this level you need to continue developing endurance, threshold power, climbing and sprinting. Remember to allow adequate recovery so that you're fresh enough to complete the hard sessions, and build in specific elements to peak for particular goals, such as hill climbing or sprinting. A road racer's typical training week is shown opposite.

The next step from this level is to increase quality and quantity further; to do this you may consider getting your own personal coach. Having somebody else on board will give you a fresh perspective and can also help with motivation – you're not just accountable to yourself. A good coach will be able to look at personal physiological data such as heart rate and power-meter files and devise a personal training plan most suited to your strengths, weaknesses and goals.

Time trialling is the ultimate test of individual strength. There is no assistance and a rider simply has to cover the course at the fastest speed possible. You must think about pacing yourself to get the best performance over the whole distance. The more aerodynamic you can make your riding position, the less drag and air resistance you will have to combat, allowing you to turn more of your power into raw speed.

Road racers will do time trials as part of longer tours, and there are certain specialist time trials over challenging courses. Following cars are allowed and riders can be encouraged with blasts of the horn, or their 'Directeur Sportif' shouting at them through a megaphone. Some will use an earpiece for more discreet encouragement and also for the supply of information, such as time checks so that they can judge their relative progress.

A ROAD RACER'S TYPICAL TRAINING WEEK

Mon	Day off or **60 mins** blue
Tues	**3 hours** green with 4 x 10 mins yellow
Weds	**3 hours** 45 mins green then 6–8 x 1min MAX flat, progress to climbs Finish with 1 hour green
Thurs	**1 hour** blue/ green Think of high cadence/skills Progress to sprints e.g. 20 mins warm up, 6 x 20 secs, cool down.
Fri	**2 hours** 45 mins green then e.g. 8, 8, 8 progressing to 12, 10, 8 amber with 8–10 mins rest Cool down green/blue
Sat	**1–2 hours** green
Sun	**Race or 3 hours** with 1 hour green, then 5 x 6 mins yellow, building into amber Progress to sprinting at end.

15-HOUR PLAN

WEEK	Mon	Tues	Weds	Thurs	Fri	Sat	Sun
1	Day off	3 hours green	3 hours 45 mins green then 6 x 1 min MAX flat Finish with 1 hour green	45 mins blue/green Skill session	2 hours 45 mins green then 8, 8, 8 amber with 8–10 mins rest Cool down green/blue	60 mins green	Race or 3 hours with 1 hour green, then 4 x 5 min hills yellow, building into amber at end
2	Day off or 30 mins blue	3 hours green with 2 x 10 mins yellow	3 hours 45 mins green then 6 x 1min MAX flat Finish with 1 hour green	45 mins blue/green Skill session	2 hours 45 mins green then 8, 8, 8 amber with 8–10 mins rest Cool down green/blue	60 mins green	Race or 3 hours with 1 hour green, then 4 x 6 min hills yellow, building into amber at end
3	Day off or 30 mins blue	3 hours green with 2 x 10 mins yellow	3 hours 45 mins green then 8 x 1 min MAX flat Finish with 1 hour green	60 mins blue/green Skill session	2 hours 45 mins green then 8, 8, 8 amber with 8–10 mins rest Cool down green/blue	90 mins green	Race or 3 hours with 1 hour green, then 4 x 6 min hills yellow, building into amber at end
4	Day off or 45 mins blue	3 hours green with 3 x 10 mins yellow	3 hours 45 mins green then 8 x 1 min MAX flat Finish with 1 hour green	60 mins blue/green Skill session	2 hours 45 mins green then 10, 8, 8 amber with 8–10 mins rest Cool down green/blue	90 mins green	Race or 3 hours with 1 hour green, then 4 x 6 min hills yellow, building into amber into sprint at end
5	Day off or 45 mins blue	3 hours green with 3 x 10 mins yellow	3 hours 45 mins green then 6–8 x 1 min MAX hill Finish with 1 hour green	60 mins Warm up, then 4–6 sprints Cool down	2 hours 45 mins green then 10, 8, 8 amber with 8–10 mins rest Cool down green/blue	120 mins green	Race or 3 hours with 1 hour green, then 4 x 6 min hills yellow, building into amber into sprint at end
6	Day off or 1 hour blue	3 hours green with 4 x 10 mins yellow	3 hours 45 mins green then 6-8 x 1 min MAX hill Finish with 1 hour green	60 mins Warm up, then 4–6 sprints Cool down	2 hours 45 mins green then 10, 10, 8 amber with 8–10 mins rest Cool down green/blue	120 mins green	Race or 3 hours with 1 hour green, then 5 x 6 min hills yellow. building into amber into sprint at end
7	Day off or 1 hour blue	3 hours green with 4 x 10 mins yellow	3 hours 45 mins green then 6-8 x 1min MAX hill Finish with 1 hour green	60 mins Warm up, then 6–8 sprints Cool down	2 hours 45 mins green then 12, 10, 8 amber with 8–10 mins rest Cool down green/blue	120 mins green	Race or 3 hours with 1 hour green, then 5 x 6 min hills yellow, building into amber into sprint at end
8	Day off	60 mins green	2 hours green with 6 x 20 second sprints	Day off	60 mins green with 3 x 20-second sprints	Test	Rest

One of the most prestigious time trials is the Hour Record. This is ridden on the track and is basically the maximum distance ridden in exactly 60 minutes. The first male record was set in 1876 on a 'Penny Farthing'. Fausto Coppi and Eddy Merckx are amongst the holders, and in 1996 Britain's Chris Boardman rode 56.375km, but cycling's world governing body, the Union Cycliste International (UCI), then changed the rules to restrict technical advances in bike design. Czech rider Ondrej Sosenka rode 49.7km under the new rules in 2005. There have been fewer attempts by women, but Dutch rider Leontien Zijlaard-Van Moorsel covered 46.065km in 2003.

There are also time trials ridden over specific distances, a branch of the sport which is particularly popular in Britain. Events are held over 10, 25, 50 and 100 miles (approximately 16, 40, 80 and 160km), and there are also 12-hour and 24-hour time trials where the record is well over 500 miles (800 km)!

Team time trials test not just your own personal ability to get out your maximum effort, but the organisational ability of a group of riders working together. This is the ultimate pace-line!

THE TIME TRIAL BIKE AND EQUIPMENT

A time trial bike is all about stiffness and aerodynamics, and nothing to do with comfort!

- **Frame:** This is made from lightweight, stiff, aerodynamic tubing and has a very short and low head tube, allowing the handlebars to be set up very low.
- **Handlebars:** The 'tri- bars' (which take their name from 'Triathlon') come in different styles and positions and aim to keep the hands and elbows as close together as possible, to reduce the frontal area.
- **Gear levers:** These are fitted to the end of the 'skis' and allow riders to change gear without moving their hands or having to change position.
- **Brakes:** Aerodynamic brake levers are on the side bars for control when cornering or descending.
- **Wheels:** Disk wheels or four spoked wheels and deep rims are some of the options available to time triallists. These are banned from 'bunch' racing but have superior aerodynamics and can take minutes off a longer time trial.
- **Tyres/'Tubs':** Thin tyres with low rolling resistance are ideal for time trials and 'tubulars' are often used as they allow lighter wheels that do not need the added weight of the 'clincher' rims used for standard tyres.
- **Bottle cage:** Depending on the length of the time trial, you may not need a bottle and bottle cage, but if you do there are aerodynamic versions available.
- **Helmet and visor:** The helmet can be the most valuable investment for time triallists, saving up to a minute over 40km. Depending on the type of helmet that is right for you, a visor can be better than glasses.
- **Skin suit:** A seamless suit with no pockets and fabrics that reduce drag both help you go faster.
- **Over-socks:** These can also help save you seconds as they create less disturbance in the airflow than the buckles and bulky closures on most shoes.

Riding position

Time triallists aim to make the frontal area hitting the wind as small as possible to try and reduce drag. This low position can be achieved by moving the saddle slightly forwards compared to the traditional 'road' position, lowering the handlebars and using tri-bars that bring your hands, arms and elbows together. It may feel extreme, and a lot of riding in this position is needed before your muscles fully adapt to working hard like this.

Physical traits

Unless a time trial course is particularly technical, the winner will be the rider who can produce the maximum power for the required time. Strength and a high functional threshold are vitally important, but the mind also plays a large part.

Pacing is a key element in time trials: you need to start fast and then hold your pace, finishing exhausted, having given absolutely everything within yourself. They are brutal because of the effort and concentration required and you need to practise not only the physical workload but the ability to judge that effort. Try not to start too hard as you may create too

much lactic acid too soon and your body may never recover during the rest of the ride.

Find out as much as possible about the course and the likely wind direction and choose gears and equipment accordingly. Then think about pacing and where you will need to be going at full power, but also where there may be opportunities to recover while still keeping the speed high.

You can use the typical road racer's week (see p. 146) as a template for your time trial training, with one or two adjustments. You will still need to do the longer steady rides (blue and green) for the base endurance to support the higher-quality work and include threshold rides to mimic race performance. You should also develop your anaerobic fitness with one- to three-minute efforts. Make sure you have enough time to completely recover between intervals to maintain the quality of all the hard efforts in your session. The same goes for 30-second maximal efforts, which should be separated by 10-minute 'rest' periods riding at 'blue'. Incorporate these two types of intervals into your Wednesday and Friday rides and do these on your time trial bike. Other longer sessions may be done on a standard road bike if you have that alternative.

FACT

20 million bikes are owned in the UK, which means that one in three adults has one; although only six million people are regular cycle users.

TRACK RACING

Track racing takes place on banked tracks usually made from wood and built with banked curves as steep as 50 degrees to make a smooth transition from the straights to the banking, allowing the riders to take the corners at up to 60km per hour without having to ease off. You can really feel the G-force pushing you down into your bike as you take the corners at full speed!

THE BIKE

Track bikes are built for pure speed; with one fixed gear and no brakes, riders have to control the speed with their pedalling.

Events are either time trials against the clock, individually or as a team, on time-trial-style bikes searching for aerodynamics and speed, or eye to eye against your rivals in matched sprints or bunched racing, where the tactical games of cat and mouse can often mean that the clever rider can win over the strongest!

SPRINT EVENTS

These are the explosive events of track racing, over short distances and requiring huge amounts of power. As there are no hills involved, the need for a good power-to-weight ratio is not as important as in road racing; sheer strength and speed, along with track craft and a tactical mind, are the keys to success.

- **Sprint:** Riders qualify with a flying 200m time trial to create the seedings, and then match sprints of two to four riders, where the winners progress to the next round. The heats are sometimes decided on one ride, and the later stages (from the quarter-finals onwards) usually over the best of three rides. Here tactics and bike handling are important as riders try to make full use of the acceleration of the bankings in the dash for the line.

- **Keiren:** This event was created in Japan. Six to eight riders start together, paced by a motorised bike – the 'derny'. This gradually speeds up while riders fight for the best position, and then as it pulls off the track with around 600m to go, the riders race to the line, using the high speeds generated by the motor pacing and tactics to win.

- **500m/1000m:** This is an individual time trial where the rider starts from an electronically controlled starting gate and has to complete the distance as fast as possible.

- **Team sprint:** This is for teams of two or three riders, who start in a set order. The first rider completes his or her lap and then swings off to allow the next one to take over. The first rider's race is now over and they ride high on the banking while the team continues. The next rider leads for their lap and swings off to allow the final rider to take over and complete the final lap. It's important to keep together as the final rider has to stay in the shelter of his or her team mates to try and save as much energy as possible until their lap.

ENDURANCE EVENTS

These events require different physical characteristics as riders need to sustain high power for longer periods of time.

- **3km/4km pursuit:** Two riders start at opposite sides of the track from an electronic starting gate, with the aim of completing the distance in the fastest possible time or catching, and therefore eliminating, their opponent.

- **Team pursuit:** Like the individual pursuit, two teams of three or four riders start at opposite sides of the track, with one rider nominated as the starter, who begins from the electronic starting gate. The teams ride in aerodynamic formation, swapping turns at setting the pace and recovering while trying to complete the distance in the fastest time possible. If one team catches the other before the full distance, that team is the winner. The finishing time is taken on the third rider crossing the finish line, and it's possible in team pursuits of four riders for one to drop off the back before the end. If this happens, that rider cannot rejoin the team.

- **Scratch race:** Similar to road racing, the riders begin together and the first rider across the line at the end of the race is the winner. Due to the short tracks it's possible for breakaway riders to 'gain a lap' if they are fast enough to catch the back of the bunch. They may then continue to ride in the bunch until there are ten or five laps to go, when the 'lapped' riders are signalled to race to an early finish. This allows the remaining riders who are on the same 'lap' to contest the finish without being confused with the lapped riders. There is no limit on how many laps a rider can gain on the bunch. There is an opportunity for team tactics in scratch races where two or more riders may ride for the same team.

- **Points race:** This is a massed-start race, and at regular intervals, usually every ten laps, a whistle is blown to signal that points are to be awarded in an intermediate sprint. The first four riders to cross the line are awarded 5, 3, 2 and 1 point. This continues throughout the race, with the winner being the rider who has accumulated the most points, not necessarily the first rider across the line at the end of the race. Due to the short tracks, each rider who breaks away and 'gains a lap' on the bunch is awarded an extra 20 points; similarly, 20 points are deducted from riders who 'lose a lap'. If some riders have gained a lap when the whistle is blown for the next sprint, all the riders in the bunch can compete for points, regardless of whether they are on the same 'lap' as the leaders. If two or more riders are tied on points at the end of the race, their position crossing the finish line will determine the winner.

- **Madison:** Teams of two riders take part in this event, which is like a points race relay. There are sprints at regular intervals, usually every twenty laps, and one rider per team is always 'active' in the race. The changeover takes place by using a hand-sling action that transfers the speed of the active rider to the rider who is entering the race and taking over the 'active' role. When it's safe, the 'un-active' rider then moves to the top of the banking and cycles gently round to recover and prepare for the next changeover, which usually takes place every time the fast-racing bunch catches up the slow-moving rider, who swoops down the banking to gain speed and then performs the hand-sling manoeuvre to take up the role of being active in the race again. As in the points race, points won in intermediate sprints are totalled at the end of the race and added to any 20-point bonuses for 'gaining a lap'. The winners are the pair with the most points. Both riders need to have a good tactical awareness to keep up with the events of the race and the positions of the different teams each time they enter and leave the active race. It is also possible to try and combine riders' strengths by matching a strong endurance rider with a fast sprinter to maximise the team's point-scoring potential.
- **Motor-pacing:** Derny motorbikes, like those used in the Keiren, are used in this event to pace one rider per derny for the whole of the race distance. The riders follow very closely, trying to maximise the shelter available in the slipstream of their derny, which has to try and drive at the fastest possible speed that the rider is able to maintain. These events are noisy because of the engines, and very, very fast!
- **Six days:** This element of track cycling is like a stage race held over six days, but it all takes place on the track. Teams of two riders race as a madison pairing each day and take part in different races throughout the six days. Races can be varied and usually include points races, scratch races and madison pursuits, where one rider of the team will start, and instead of completing the whole distance alone, the team mates change over with a hand sling, the second rider then continuing to complete the distance. Points are awarded for the result at the end of each race. If a team gains a lap in a six-day, the lap automatically places that team in first position, regardless of their points total. Then, if two or more teams finish on the same lap, the winner is decided by the team with the highest points total.

Training for track cycling is very specific. You will still do aerobic endurance rides on the road, and you can then incorporate maximal sprints (red), anaerobic intervals up to several minutes (amber) and longer threshold rides (yellow). You will want to get as much track time as possible and you'll need to learn the handling skills for riding with so many riders racing so close together at such high speeds. Speak to the coaches at your track session and they will help you devise a training plan suited to your own fitness levels and available track time.

FACT

The first two-wheeled rider-propelled machine was invented by a German, Baron Karl de Drais de Sauerbrun, around 1818. It was made entirely of wood.

OFF-ROAD RIDING

For those of you without access to a track and looking for something away from the tarmac, there are a number of off-road specialties with a keen competitive element.

CYCLO-CROSS

Cyclo-cross is an autumn and winter sport, and is used by many 'roadies' as a way to keep fit out of season. Races often take place in local parks and are up to an hour long. Courses are generally made up of short laps which includes obstacles over which you may be able to 'bunny-hop' or you may have to dismount. There are often steeply banked sections where you have to shoulder your bike and run.

Its origins are closer to road racing than mountain biking, and a cyclo-cross bike is similar to a road bike. The only real difference is extra frame clearances and cantilever-style brakes, both adaptations designed to avoid narrow gaps clogging up with mud. They also have chunky-tread tyres and lower gears to cope with sticky conditions.

If you wish to train specifically for cyclo-cross, then practice the skills of dismounting/remounting and running with the bike. Fitness training will be much the same as for road riding, with blue/green rides for recovery and endurance and amber rides in preparation for racing, which will be time-trial-style all-out hour-long threshold efforts. You'll also need higher-intensity intervals to develop power for sprints or short, sharp climbs.

If you do ride cyclo-cross as part of your off-season road training programme, you'll find it can help you with motivation during the long, wet, cold winter months, and should improve your bike-handling skills.

MOUNTAIN BIKING

Modern mountain bikes began developing in 1970s USA. Bigger knobbly tyres on smaller wheels, straight handlebars, smaller and more compact frames and the development of suspension have seen them able to tackle increasingly difficult terrain.

As in cyclo-cross, handling skills are at a premium in mountain biking; in fact in downhill competition they are the key factor because endurance fitness plays a relatively small part in the discipline. Many skills are required that are not needed on the road: for instance, the ability to ride over large 'drop-offs'. Greater all-over body strength is required to handle the bike.

- **Cross-country mountain biking** is closest to road racing. These are mass-start races with endurance fitness being a key factor, in addition to the off-road skills required. In fact many cross-country racers will do much of their endurance training on the road to get more consistent steady-state riding. Cross country requires a good power-to-weight ratio; indeed, because of the short and very steep climbs, developing maximum power output will provide a big advantage. The nature of the course often means there are short stretches where very-high-intensity effort is required. These sections are spread out across the race, and there is far less of the steady-paced riding found in a road event. Training the body for those short, sharp efforts and quick recovery should be one of the elements of your training. While most cross-country races feature several laps of a course and last between one and two hours, there are also MTB stage races, while Marathon XC is a point-to-point form of off-road racing of up to 100km.
- **Enduro:** If stamina is one of your strengths, you may consider entering an Enduro. These events last for either 12 or 24 hours and feature teams of riders. The winners are the riders or teams who complete the most number of laps.
- **Dual slalom** is similar to downhill skiing, with two riders going head to head on technical man-made courses. They race on identical side-by-side tracks which include jumps and banked corners.
- **Dual races** have the same format but with both riders on the same track.
- **4X**, as the name suggests, has four riders competing and is a

mix of downhill and BMX (a long-established branch of cycle sport which has now been given Olympic recognition). Raced on tiny framed bikes on circuits of around 350m, eight riders compete in each round and there are normally heats, quarter-finals, semi-finals and the final.

○ **Downhill** is mountain biking's version of time trialling, with added adrenaline! Held on steep, rugged slopes, races last up to three minutes and include a great deal of technical difficulty. Downhill bikes have full suspension with up to 20cm travel on the front shocks, and 25cm or more at the rear. Frames, of course, have to be fairly bomb-proof so are relatively heavy; this is not a great issue since gravity is mainly in your favour! Downhill bikes are also equipped with disc brakes, and riders tend to use full body armour. Courses can feature 3m drops and 12m jumps, and to ride them fast needs great mental ability as well as strength, fitness and immense skill.

Even in some of the downhill events, such as dual slalom or 4X, there will be short bursts of speed required, so your training should include anaerobic intervals and sessions aimed at developing maximum power.

If you have developed outstanding off-road bike handling, there are even competitions for you to show off your fancy tricks. Freeride is all about negotiating jumps, drops and ramps as smoothly as possible, with judges awarding points for style.

There really is something for everyone who wants to challenge themselves on a bike, whatever yours is, do it with passion and make sure you enjoy it!

I hope you've found this book helpful and that it inspires you to get more out of your cycling. Of course there's always more to learn and there are plenty of sources of further information and help. This final section gives some advice and information about cycling organisations and a glossary of terms.

PART FOUR

BIKE KNOWLEDGE

TAKING IT FURTHER

JOINING A CLUB

If you've decided to enter a race or want to share in the fun and excitement of cycling with other like-minded people, consider joining a local club where you will find support and advice, regardless of your ability level. Cycling clubs offer valuable knowledge and assistance to help you get the most out of your riding. There will be other riders to share your passion and plenty of experience to help you improve and learn more about the sport.

Clubs usually have regular rides catering for a range of riders, from beginners up to racing level. They plan suitable routes based on ability, so you don't have to worry about where to go; just turn up and enjoy the safety and security that comes with an organised ride on the road. You should be able to find a group that suits your speed, but which at times will also stretch you a little and help you to keep improving.

By being around other cyclists you can easily ask for advice and support and find people to help and share in your personal goals. You can also find out more about technical aspects of cycling and keep up to date with new equipment and components, new places to ride and the latest news of the cycling world.

TIP

As well as joining a club consider being a member of one of your national racing or touring bodies. This can bring many benefits, including accident and travel insurance.

The easiest way to find a club is probably to pop into your local bike shop and ask about groups in your area — where they meet and when. If there are several in your area, try them all and see which seems to suit you best. Alternatively, contact your national governing body for a list of clubs, and also what other structures there are to help you develop your cycling. For example, if you live in the United Kingdom, British Cycling have a development programme which includes a network of 'Go-Ride' clubs aimed at developing young riders. They also have a Talent ID scheme to find and guide talented cyclists through to becoming World and Olympic champions, and a Talent Team which has enthusiastic, experienced and inspirational coaches to take riders to the highest level.

FINDING A COACH

If you would like some specific advice tailored to your ability and goals, a coach could help you get the most quality out of the time you have available to ride or help you prepare specifically for your targets. Qualified coaches are able to call on their own experience and knowledge of the latest coaching methods. They can advise and help plan everything, from a whole season to your week's training, with the details of each ride you should complete. They also have the advantage of not being the ones doing the training and can be very supportive in seeing the bigger picture of your development; you could easily become caught up in the 'more is better' approach, which can lead to over-training.

RESOURCES

INTERNATIONAL ORGANISATIONS

Union Cycliste International (UCI)
(The governing body for world cycle sport)
Ch. de la Mêlée 12
1860 Aigle
Switzerland
Tel: +41 2 446 85 811
Web: www.uci.ch/english/index.htm

European Cyclists' Federation (ECF)
(A campaigning group which lobbies the European Parliament)
Rue Joseph II 166
1000 Brussels
Belgium
Tel: +32 2 234 38 74
Web: www.ecf.com

International Mountain Biking Association (IMBA)
(A non-profit association which aims to create, enhance and preserve great trail experiences for mountain bikers worldwide)
PO Box 7578
Boulder
CO 80306
USA
Tel: +1 888 442 4622
Web: www.imba.com

SOME NATIONAL ASSOCIATIONS AND ORGANISATIONS

Australia
Cycling Australia
(Australian Cycling Federation)
PO Box 7183
Bass Hill
NSW 2197
Tel: +61 2 9644 3002
Web: www.cycling.org.au

Australian Time Trials Association
Web: www.atta.asn.au

Bicycle Federation of Australia
PO Box 499
Civic Square
ACT 2608
Tel: +61 2 6249 6761
Web: www.bfa.asn.au

Belgium
Royale Ligue Velocipedique Belge (KBWB)
Globelaan 49
1190 Vorst
Tel: +32 (0) 2 349 19 11
Web: www.kbwb-rlvb.be

Federation Cycliste Wallonie – Bruxelles
Avenue du Globe, 49/1
B-1190 Brussels
Tel: +32 2 349 19 20
Web: www.fcwb.be

Canada
Canadian Cycling Association
Suite 203 – 2197 Riverside Drive
Ottawa
Ontario K1H 7X3
Tel: +1 613 248 1353
Web: www.canadian-cycling.com

France
Fédération Française de Cyclisme
Bat. Jean Monnet
5 rue de Rome
93561 Rosny Sous Bois
Tel: +33 (0)1 49 35 69 00
Web: www.ffc.fr

Ireland
Cycling Ireland
Kelly Roche
619 North Circular Road
Dublin 1
Tel: +353 (1) 855 1522
Web: www.cyclingireland.ie

Italy
Federazione Ciclistica Italiana
Stadio Olimpico – Curva Nord
00194 – Roma
Tel: +39 (0)6 3685 1
Web: www.federciclismo.it

Netherlands
Koninklijke Nederlandsche Wielren Unie
Wattbaan 31–49
3439 ML Nieuwegein
Tel: +31 (0)30 7513300
Web: www.knwu.nl

New Zealand
BikeNZ
PO Box 38170
Wellington Mail Centre
Lower Hutt 5045
Tel: +64 (04) 560 0333
Web: www.bikenz.org.nz

South Africa
Cycling South Africa
Web: cms.cyclingsa.com

United Kingdom
British Cycling
Stuart Street
Manchester M11 4DQ
Tel: +44 (0)161 274 2000
Web: www.britishcycling.org.uk

Cyclists Touring Club (CTC)
Parklands
Railton Road
Guildford GU2 9JX
Tel: +44 (0)870 873 0060
Web: www.ctc.org.uk

Road Time Trials Council
Web: www.cyclingtimetrials.org.uk

Women's Cycle Racing Association
Web: www.wcra.org.uk

United States of America
USA Cycling
1 Olympic Plaza
Colorado Springs
CO 80909
Tel: +1 719 866 4581
Web: www.usacycling.org

League of American Bicyclists
1612 K Street NW
Suite 800
Washington
DC 20006-2850
Tel: +1 (202) 822-1333
Web: www.bikeleague.org

COACHING RESOURCES
Association of British Cycling Coaches
Web: www.abcc.co.uk

The Coaching Association of Canada
141 Laurier Avenue West
Suite 300
Ottawa
Ontario K1P 5J3
Tel: +1 613 235 5000
Web: www.coach.ca

SOME TOURING WEBSITES
cyclingaroundtheworld.nl/wtx
www.josiedew.co.uk

SOME SPORTIVE WEBSITES
Global
www.ucigoldenbike.com

France
www.letapedutour.com
www.sportcommunication.com

Italy
www.granfondopinarello.com/index.php
www.faustocoppi.net
www.gazzetta.it/challenge
www.maratona.it
www.eroica.it

UK
www.cyclosport.org
www.etapecaledonia.co.uk
www.etapedudales.co.uk
www.dragonride.co.uk
www.tourofwessex.com

GLOSSARY

Adenosine triphosphate (ATP) – A compund found in every cell in the body, it transports chemical energy within cells for metabolism.

Aerobic – Exercise that uses oxygen in energy production. This occurs at lower intensities.

Amenorrhea – The cessation of menstrual periods for at least three months; this can be associated with stress, over-training and poor nutrition.

Anaerobic – Energy production without oxygen, allowing short periods of high-intensity exercise.

Anaerobic threshold – The point at which the aerobic energy system can no longer fulfil the body's demands for adenosine triphosphate.

Basal metabolic rate (BMR) – The amount of energy expended while at rest in a neutrally temperate environment. It is the minimum calorific requirement to sustain life in a resting individual.

Body Mass Index (BMI) – Used to estimate body composition, based on height and weight.

Bonk – Also 'hunger knock' or 'hitting the wall'. The condition when a cyclist runs out of energy, resulting in a major performance drop.

Bottom bracket – The joint at the bottom of the bike frame through which the cranks are joined.

Branched-chain amino acids – A group of amino acids that help to maintain muscle tissue; they are also needed during times of physical stress and intense exercise.

Break (or break-away) – The lone rider or small group of riders who are riding ahead of the main pack.

Bridge – To 'Bridge a gap' is to cross from one group of riders to another, normally to catch a break.

Bunny hop – Jumping the bike over obstacles with both wheels off the ground.

Cadence – The number of revolutions of the crankset per minute.

Calorie (kcal) – The amount of heat (energy) needed to increase the temperature of 1kg of water by 1°C and used to measure food energy.

Cardio-respiratory – Relating to heart and lungs.

Cardio-vascular – Relating to heart and blood vessels.

Cartilage – Strong but non-elastic connective tissue that prevents friction,

acts as a shock absorber and also adds structure to the skeleton.

Cassette – The group or 'cluster' of gear cogs on the rear hub. Also known as a 'block'.

Clincher – The most common tyre, it has beads which hook over the wheel rim and a separate inner tube.

Core stability – The core muscles lie deep within the trunk of the body and create a firm foundation for co-ordinated movement of the legs and arms.

Crankset – The cranks and chain ring plus bottom bracket which form the front part of a bike's transmission.

Creatine phosphate – An important energy store in skeletal muscle which can help form adenosine triphosphate.

Criterium (or Crit) – A multi-lap race held on a short circuit typified by tight corners, often on closed-off city-centre streets.

Cross-training – Incorporating different sports (e.g. running) into your cycle training.

Cyclo-sportive – see Sportive

Derailleur – The common form of gear changer which uses levers and wires to push the chain from cog to cog.

Domestique – A road racer who works solely for the benefit of his or her team and leader. The French domestique literally translates as 'servant'.

DOMS – Delayed onset muscle soreness.

Drafting – see Slipstream.

Echelon – a form of paceline used to get maximum draught in a crosswind.

Ergogenic – Any external influence which can positively affect physical or mental performance.

Fixie – A fixed gear with one cog; freewheeling is not possible.

Fork – Two blades through the head tube of the bike frame which holds the front wheel and connects to the handlebars.

Frameset – The bike frame and fork, either with or without the headset.

Freewheeling – Moving on the bike without pedalling, for example downhill.

Functional threshold heart rate (FThr) – The heart rate associated with the maximum pace a cyclist can sustain for a one-hour time trial.

Functional threshold power (FTp) – The maximum average wattage that a cyclist can sustain for a one-hour time trial.

General classification (GC) – The overall standing in a stage race after the accumulation of daily finishing times.

Glycaemic Index – The ranking of carbohydrates on a scale from 0 to 100 according to the extent to which they raise blood sugar levels after eating.

Glycogen – The form in which carbohydrate is stored in the body, usually within muscle.

Granny gear – The largest chain ring and smallest cog, a very small gear for the steepest of climbs.

Group set – A collection of parts to go with a frameset. Group sets include gears, cranks, chain, brakes and seat post, but not usually pedals.

Haematocrit – Ratio by volume of red blood cells to whole blood.

Headset – The bearings within the head tube to which the forks are attached.

Heart rate (HR) – The number of times the heart beats in one minute.

Heart rate reserve (HRR) – A term used to describe the difference between a person's measured or predicted maximum heart rate and resting heart rate.

Hub – The central part of the wheel connected to the rim by the spokes.

Hybrid – A cross between a road bike and a mountain bike, often used for leisure riding or commuting.

Interval training – Short periods of high-intensity work separated by low-intensity recovery periods. This allows a higher total of quality training within the total session.

Jump – In off-road riding this is 'catching air', on the road a jump is an attack designed to drop other rides.

Kermesse – A criterium-style race popular in Northern Europe. Named after the French word for 'village fair' (which is when they were traditionally held).

Lactate threshold (also known as anaerobic threshold) – The point during exercise when lactate in the blood accumulates quicker than it can be dissipated. Raising the lactate threshold is a key goal for cycling fitness.

Lactic acid – Produced by the body as part of the anaerobic energy system. Not a 'waste' product as often thought, but does cause pain in muscles.

Lead out – A sprinter may have several specialised domestiques to 'lead them out' by riding in front of them to build up speed whilst the sprinter saves energy for the final push to the line.

Ligament – Fibrous connective tissue which joins bones together.

Maximum heart rate (MHR) – The highest heart rate a person can attain, often estimated as 220 minus age, though this can be quite inaccurate.

Metabolic rate – The speed of metabolism (production of energy to support body function).

Off the back – Riders who have been dropped and are trailing behind the main field.

Osteoporosis – A condition where low bone mass leads to bones becoming brittle and susceptible to fractures.

Over-training – Excessive training without adequate recovery, causing a reversal in fitness and leading to health problems.

Paceline – Where riders race behind each other in a cooperative line in order to benefit from the slipstream effect. Riders take it in turns to be at the front.

Pannier – A specially designed cycle bag that hangs on a rack either side of the wheels.

Peloton – From the French, 'the bunch' or 'the pack', it is the large main group in a road race.

Physical activity quotient (PAQ) – The amount of calories used on a daily basis in addition to your basal metabolic rate.

Prime (pronounced 'preem') – Points, seconds bonus or prize awarded for particular climbs or sprint points along the course of a race.

Progressive overload – The gradual increase of stress placed upon the body during training. It stimulates the body to regenerate and become stronger and fitter.

Reps – Short for Repetitions of an exercise (sprints on the bike or lifts in the weights room). Reps make up sets.

Resistance training – A form of strength training in which each effort is performed against a specific opposing force generated by resistance.

Resting heart rate (RHR) – The number of beats per minute at absolute rest, ideally recorded first thing in the morning.

Revolutions per minute (RPM) – The number of full rotations completed by the pedals in one minute; used to measure cadence or leg speed.

Rollers – Allow you to ride a bike whilst stationary, but without the resistance supplied by a turbo trainer. Good for pre-race warm-ups.

Slipstream – Slipstreaming or drafting is where cyclists shelter behind another rider to reduce the effort required to maintain a certain speed.

Soft pedal – Turning the cranks but not actually applying power.

Spin – Pedalling lower gears at a high cadence (as oppose to 'pushing' big gears).

Spinning – High-intensity exercise class on stationary bikes. Held in a gym, the sessions feature music and a group instructor.

Sportive – An organised mass-participation ride typically held on challenging terrain. Although timed, they are not races.

Sprocket – A gear cog on the rear cassette.

Strength training – The use of resistance to muscular contraction in order to build the strength, anaerobic endurance and size of skeletal muscles.

Submaximal – Below maximum effort or intensity. An interval where you hold something back.

Tendon – Strong fibrous tissue that connects muscle to bone.

Tempo – Riding quickly, but not flat out.

Triathlon – Triathlons combine swimming, cycling and running over varying distances. The 'Ironman' features a 2.4-mile (3.86 km) swim, a 112-mile (180km) bike ride, and 26.2-mile (42 km) run.

Tubulars – A lightweight tyre that has the tube permanently sewn inside the casing. 'Tubs' are glued to the rim.

Turbo-trainer – A training device that supports the bike and provides resistance to the rear wheel, allowing stationary exercise.

Velodrome – A cycling track with banked corners.

V02 max – The highest rate of oxygen consumption attainable during maximal or exhaustive exercise. Measured in millilitres of oxygen per kilogram of body weight per minute. A key indicator of athletic fitness.

Wheel base – The distance between the centres of the two wheels. Racers usually have a more manoeuvrable short base, tourers a more stable long base.

INDEX

AND FINALLY...

On a bike you can travel up to 1037km on the energy equivalent of a single litre of petrol.

Twenty bicycles can be parked in the same space as one car.

China produces 55–60 per cent of the world's bicycles. India produces 11 per cent.

Cycling when pregnant improves cardiovascular fitness and regular exercise may ease childbirth.

In Tokyo, a bike is faster than a car for most trips of less than 50 minutes.

ACKNOWLEDGEMENTS

The publishers would like to thank the following contributors:

Raleigh for the use of their bikes on pages 124, 128 and 153.

Halfords for contributing the images on pages 28, 30 and 123.

Larry Hickmott at British Cycling for the images on pages 141 and 150.

The publishers would also like to thank Simon Hammond and John Davis for their patience and guidance on the photoshoot.

PICTURE CREDITS